DECIDE HAPPY

Less Stress. More Joy.

A Practical Guide

SUSAN DENNY HALL

Decide Happy
Less Stress More Joy-A Practical Guide

For information about this title or to order other books and/or electronic media, contact the publisher:

Susan Hall
DecideHappy.com
susanhall@DecideHappy.com

ISBNs:
979-8-9856864-0-1 (softcover)
979-8-9856864-1-8 (eBook)

Printed in the United States of America

Cover and Interior design: 1106 Design

Dedicated to Marian Denny, my mother,
who taught me that happiness is an inside job.
And that on any day, at any moment, I can *Decide*.

Table of Contents

DECIDE HAPPY
QUICK REFERENCE GUIDE

HAPPINESS IS A CONSTANT DECISION

This Quick Reference Guide will point you to the chapters and tools designed to help you with specific challenges you may be experiencing.

Every chapter of *Decide Happy* includes tools, examples, and tips for more joy in your days. Remember to stack multiple practices for multiple impact!

DECIDE HAPPY: DEFINITION OF HAPPINESS

The skills in this book will help you more consistently achieve a greater sense of:

Love and connection—in your relationships with people, animals, nature, yourself, and the world around you

Peacefulness and calm—an inner strength and state of presence and well-being. That sense of gratitude and "I've got this," no matter what life throws at you

Contribution and making a difference—leaving the day and your corner of the world a little bit better than how you found it

Moving forward—the feeling of making progress emotionally and physically, moving with purpose toward your goals

When You Feel . . .	Go to Chapter . . .	Key Tool(s)
Stuck or ready for a change	*Decide—Your Turn (2)*	Decide Practice
Overwhelmed You want to make an unfun thing better	*Stack Life in Your Favor (3)*	Three-fers One step at a time "No, thank you"
Scared, frustrated, angry, or down	*Focus (4)*	What if? Better Questions
Lonely, judged, or criticized You want better relationships with awesome people	*Choose Your People Wisely (5)*	Find Your People BOA
You need to fix a relationship rift or want more love and connection	*Clean Up Your Mess (6)*	The Letter Slay the Dragon Ditch the Blame Game Apologize/Forgive/Repeat
That Inner Critic is whispering or shouting: "I can't do this." "I'm not good enough." You want to magnify your strengths	*Be Gentle with Yourself (7)*	Silence the Inner Critic Iceberg Illusion 6-3-3
The need for more calm and less drama	*Mind Your Words (8)*	Dial down/Dial up
Let go of pain, grief, and anger	*Let It Go (9)*	Refocus

When You Feel . . .	Go to Chapter . . .	Key Tool(s)
Overwhelmed or stuck The desire to move forward	*The Power of Progress* (10)	Power Momentum Process One Step at a Time
A loss, or you're going through a tough time You want more juice in life	*Feel It All* (11)	Reflect & Journal Celebrate
You're kinda bugged or grumpy and don't know why	*Observe Your Thoughts* (12)	Digging for Truth/Crap
You need a guaranteed burst of happy You're tired of your own Pity Party You want to step up and feel fulfilled	*Be Kindhearted* (13)	Starfish Story One Small Act
Scattered and hectic The need to feel more connected	*Be There When You're There* (14)	One Person, One Thing at a Time
Stressed out You want to cultivate a sense of calm	*Clear the Clutter* (15)	The Daily Ten Three Good Rules
Any time you want a quick hit of happy You're going through a tough time	*Gratitude* (16)	Daily Questions

When You Feel ...	Go to Chapter ...	Key Tool(s)
Out of control, frustrated The need for a greater sense of calm and to set yourself up for success	***Control*** *(17)*	Sweet Spot Three Better Ways
You want to see things more positively, from a better perspective	***Meaning*** *(18)*	Event-Meaning-Behavior SAC
A desire to become a better version of yourself	***Identity*** *(19)*	Change your label-behavior-life
You want to increase joy and love and feel more present	***Savor the Moment*** *(20)*	Daily Rituals
You need courage, confidence, energy, strength	***Stand Up Straight*** *(21)*	Channel Your Inner Rock Star Move!
A desire to create lasting change A longing to be even better than you are today	***The Habit of Happiness*** *(22)*	Action Plan

1. Decide Happy

"You've always had the power, my dear.
You just had to learn it for yourself."
—Glinda, the Good Witch
The Wizard of Oz

What does it take for you to feel happy?

I'm guessing that you picked up this book because you know, deep down inside, that life has the potential to be even more joyful for you and your loved ones. And I'm also guessing that you're ready to make a change.

- Maybe you're going through a particularly stressful time right now, with tough things stacking up and feeling uncomfortably, or unbearably, heavy.

- Maybe you're taking stock of your life and realizing the days are going by far too quickly.

* Maybe you're going through a transition and feeling unmoored.

* Maybe you're "fine." You know, things aren't terrible. You really can't complain. But maybe you're thinking, *"Is this it? I mean, shouldn't life be something more? Shouldn't I be something more?"*

* Maybe you're tired of feeling crabby, tense, anxious, or frustrated.

* Maybe you're tired of how quickly you snap or use that harsh tone of voice with your loved ones.

* Maybe you're just tired of feeling tired.

We spend a lot of time thinking, *"I'll be happy when . . ." "I'll feel joy if . . ." "If only this happens, then I'll be happy." "If . . . then."*

What if you didn't have to wait?

You deserve every happiness in life. And yes, you already have the power. Sometimes it just takes a little extra focus and attention, a little reminder from a friend to stop and breathe and *do* the things you know to do, and maybe try out a few new things.

This book contains *real* skills to help you deal with *real* challenges in *real* life.

In these pages, you will find practical skills you can use immediately to bring more joy into your life and the lives of your loved ones. Right now, in this very moment.

Decide Happy is not about being naive, cavalier, or blindly optimistic. It's the best of what I've learned from my lifelong study of human behavior, more than two decades of experience as a Performance Coach, my own life's experiences (*including a cancer diagnosis that rocked my world)*, as well as lessons learned from some very brilliant and funny friends going through their own struggles. I practice these skills every day. Some days, I'm more successful than others. Yet when I actually use these skills and *do* the things I know, I always feel happier. Without exception.

When I look at the people I've studied, respected, and admired throughout my life, I've come to these conclusions:

1. **Happiness is a constant decision.** Happier people are happy because they *choose* to be.

2. **Happier people take specific actions**—consciously or unconsciously—to consistently use skills or practices to achieve this desired emotion. Happiness is a set of learnable skills and habits, as much as it is a mindset.

3. **Happiness takes practice.** Sometimes, when things are going our way, it feels effortless to choose happiness and take the actions necessary day in and day out. And other times? Other times, it's just really hard work.

It's easy to dismiss the happiest people with an "*Oh, they're just naive. For them, everything is rainbows and unicorns.*" Or "*They're just wired differently.*" Or "*They're just lucky. They get everything they want. They don't have the challenges that I have.*"

The truth is, if we listen and empathize with others long enough, we know that we *all* experience challenges.

* Why is it that one person can seem to walk through hell with a smile on their face?

* And yet someone else can let an entire day crumble into ruins because the alarm didn't go off, or the traffic was snarled, or a comment from their spouse over breakfast struck a nerve.

It's easier to blame other people or challenging situations for a bad mood. But people who are consistently happier in life have learned that *they* are responsible for managing and controlling their emotions, no matter what's happening around them. And they've learned to train their brains and use specific skills (consciously or unconsciously) to support their desired emotions and responses.

It's tough to choose happy if we haven't been training our minds each day before the crisis shows up. The best metaphor I can think of for adopting a happiness mindset and skill set is that it's like going to the gym. It's a journey—not a fixed destination. Do you get to go to the gym once and get the body you want? Nope, it doesn't work that way.

Happiness is like a muscle—the more you use it, the stronger it becomes. The stronger our happiness muscle, the more "muscle memory" we build, and the better equipped we are to deal with those Real Tests that life throws at us. Happiness, like working out, is a journey, a lifelong commitment to doing small things every day that keep us on our path.

The skills you will find in this book require **practice** because, just like lifting weights, playing a musical instrument, throwing a football, or creating a work of art, life demands that we continuously *practice* these skills and build the habits needed to achieve the results we want.

Let me define what I mean by "happiness." The skills in *Decide Happy* will help you more consistently achieve a greater sense of:

Love and connection—in your relationships with people, animals, nature, yourself, and the world around you

Peacefulness and calm—an inner strength and state of presence and well-being. That sense of gratitude and "I've got this," no matter what life throws at you

Contribution and making a difference—leaving the day and your corner of the world a little bit better than how you found it

Moving forward—the feeling of making progress emotionally and physically, moving with purpose toward your goals

We all need tools for dealing with stressful situations. Whether it's a health scare, a global pandemic, a job transition, a crossroad in a relationship, a crisis with a significant other, child, or aging parent, the car behind you didn't stop for the light, the tree fell on the roof—it is NOT the event that controls our emotions. It's what we tell ourselves about that event that drives our emotions and what we do about it. And, let's face it: as beautiful and as magical as life is, if we live long enough and love enough people, we *will* experience stressful times.

I knew all of this, of course. I knew I had the skills to manage difficult situations. I *teach* these skills to other people. I just never expected to be tested so relentlessly when my world turned completely upside down. Within one, 365-day year:

1. I was diagnosed with a one-in-a-million bone tumor that resulted in the amputation of my tailbone and 2½ vertebrae, along with the accompanying nerves, in my lower spine.

2. Two months later, my husband Tim, also healthy and fit his whole life, landed in the hospital for an unforeseen heart procedure.

3. Six weeks after that, while on vacation celebrating progress on our recoveries, I was in a freak accident and shattered my shoulder in five places, severing the "ball" of my shoulder from the bone of my upper arm and splintering it into four pieces.

4. That same year, my beloved dog, Chili Pepper, slipped his collar and ran out into the path of a speeding SUV,

which struck and killed him instantly. The driver never stopped.

5. My father fell and broke his hip for the third time, landing him permanently in a wheelchair.

It was too much.

In that one *Year That Shall Not Be Named*, I experienced the greatest fear, the greatest pain, and the greatest sorrow that I had experienced in all the decades of my life leading up to it. That year in my life challenged me to use every skill, channel every emotional muscle I had. But even that wasn't enough.

This time, I was in over my head.

I needed to quickly learn and use new skills to manage a whole different level of fear and stress. I was *desperate* to manage the thing that was causing me the most distress in this situation. And, no, I don't mean the tumor on my spine. I needed every emotional and mental tool possible to manage that three-pound thing between my ears—my brain. Because my goal was not just to survive—but to *thrive*. And to do that, I had to figure out how to find joy during what felt like an impossibly dark time.

Have you experienced times when it felt like the difficult events of your life were unfairly and overwhelmingly stacking up against you?

Times when you were called to rely on a greater strength, a greater faith, a greater hope, a greater version of yourself?

Here's what I want you to know: That very same year, with all of its tragedy and pain, I experienced countless moments of joy. I was brought to tears almost daily by acts of profound kindness and love from unexpected people at the most unexpected times. Being happy is easy when things are rolling right along the way we want them to. The challenge is in deciding to be happy when everything around us feels like it's falling apart. The challenge is in deciding to be happy when *we* feel like we're falling apart.

The single *Most Terrible and Stressful Thing* I've experienced in my life happened to be a cancer diagnosis. Maybe you've had a health scare as well. But maybe your MTST was a divorce or a difficult breakup, the loss or suffering of a loved one, a financial crisis. . . . You are no doubt painfully aware of what it is. So, while I share a handful of stories of how I dealt with the stress of cancer, you can just as easily substitute your own MTST. The skills and happiness practices work just as well, regardless of what might be freaking you out or dimming your joy.

How to Get the Most Out of This Book

"The algorithm for getting happier is actually relatively simple. The biggest mistake that people make is they wish that they were happier, but they don't work for it."
—Arthur C. Brooks

Decide Happy was intentionally designed to be read in "bite-sized" chapters to make it easy for you to use and enjoy.

Each chapter is organized into three sections:

1. **Happiness Skills**—20 skills to help you develop habits for more joy in your life, the lives of your loved ones, and the world around you.

2. **Tools**—to help you navigate rocky terrain along your life's journey, see the path forward, and tap into your own unique fabulousness every step of the way.

3. **Practices**—a thought-provoking exercise at the end of each chapter to help you be your most *loving, calm, moving-forward, contributing best.*

Be sure to check out the ***Decide Happy Quick Reference Guide*** for a summary of all the skills, tools, and practices. This way, you can focus on what's most important to you and customize your own journey through the book.

To get the most out of reading this:

1. Grab a notebook or journal and your beverage of choice. Make yourself comfortable.

2. Pick and choose the chapters that capture your attention. Or, start at the beginning and read sequentially. Read for ten minutes at a time or from cover to cover. Read however you like!

3. Check out the ***Decide Happy Quick Reference Guide.*** Select the one or two that stand out to you, and focus on using those skills. Or choose to practice one Happiness Skill a day, a week, a month.

4. However you read this book—*and this is Very Important:*

DO the Happiness Practices at the end of each chapter.

They are short and thought-provoking. I know through my experience as a leadership trainer and coach that changing human behavior is hard work. If you're a parent, you know that already!

KNOW-ing something and actually DO-ing the thing we know to do, are two very different things. You won't get a different result if you just think about it. To get a different outcome, we have to DO things a little differently. You'll never learn how to ski, or golf, or play tennis by just reading, watching videos, or thinking about it. You have to apply what you've learned by getting out there and actually DO-ing it.

Developing a Happiness mindset and skill set is the same. It's in the DO-ing, the "practicing," where you will learn the most about yourself and get the most value. I promise, they are small steps that will add up to Big Things.

Bonus Tip:

Using just one of the twenty skills consistently will help you manage stress and tap into greater levels of happiness. But stacking and using multiple skills? That's a sure recipe for more joy in your life.

My heartfelt wish is that these Happiness Skills and Practices remind you of the strength and happiness muscle you already possess and help you as you create the masterpiece that is your own journey of life, with all of its mystery and magic.

At any moment, you can decide.

Susan

So, are you ready, my friend?
Okay, let's get started!
But first, let me tell you a little story . . .

A Little Story

"The Key to Life is how well you deal with Plan B."
—Stephen Dias

"Dammit!" I blurted as I watched the sign for my exit speed past for the second time.

"You did it again, Susan. Pay attention!"

I braced my hands on the steering wheel to steady them and tried straightening my back, feeling that oppressive weight staking its familiar, unwelcome spot on my chest.

"This is just too hard," I sighed. *I can't do this.*

Out of all of the staggering things I had confronted in the two weeks since my cancer diagnosis, telling my family was unexpectedly high on the list. I dreaded the task in front of me, hating the thought of causing pain to my loved ones. I had prepared my talk as well as any business presentation, with notes and research. I even had a diagram. I practiced it again now as I continued the three-hour drive to my parents' home, more mindful of the exit signs this time.

Soon after, I sat in my parents' living room with my family and waited for the right moment to drop the bomb. **FYI—there is no right moment.** I took a deep breath and began my story, painting the most optimistic picture of the situation. Not just because that's who I am, but, if I act like I'm okay, maybe they will believe me. And maybe, just maybe, if I act okay hard enough, they will not only believe me, but maybe I'll believe me, and I'll actually be okay.

I had let my brothers and sister-in-law know beforehand, and I could feel the positive energy they were sending me as I prepared to break my parents' hearts.

I knew how it would go. My dad, the scientist, was a rock. A man short on words but long on action, none of us ever doubted for a minute how much he loved us. He would be strong and stoic. And Mom? Mom, I was worried about. She might just fall apart.

I gave my speech and took a deep breath, waiting for their reactions. My dad, true to form, was quiet as he took it all in.

"But it isn't cancer, is it?" he finally asked.

"Yes," I exhaled. "It is."

His eyes immediately welled up. That broke my heart.

Mom, in contrast—who wears her heart on her sleeve and her emotions close to the surface—didn't fall apart at all. She got strong. Mother Bear strong.

"What's the plan?" she asked.

I told her of my impending kick-butt surgery and the possible scenarios that might play out afterwards. She nodded and looked straight at me, eyes narrowed decisively.

"Susan," she said, "you will handle this the same way you handle all the other difficult things in life. One foot in front of the other, looking ahead. That's who you are."

I choked up then. I wanted so desperately to believe her, but I wasn't sure anymore. Fear loomed so dark and heavy that it seemed to swallow all the air in the room, including my strength, my voice. It was my older brother, John, who broke the silence.

"Do you think it might be because of the Denny Head?"

Steve, my younger brother, started in surprise. Understanding dawning, he quickly sat up and leaned in.

"Yeah—I mean, it could be the weight of that head pressing on the spine. You know, causing some kind of extra stress or something."

So on this particular day, after calmly breaking the news that there was an exceptionally rare type of bone tumor growing at the base of my spine, leave it to my brothers to find a way to use humor to break the tension.

I flashed back to a family get-together, with Steve wondering out loud, "Did you ever notice how Tim's head is so much smaller than ours in photos?"

My husband had rolled his eyes, prepared to once again defend his cranium that had, willingly, married into my family.

"My head is perfectly normal. It's you Dennys that all have freakishly large heads."

With the gauntlet thrown, that evening had quickly unraveled with all of us racing to find Mom's ancient measuring tape.

My family's banter brought me back to the present. It felt like a gift, that humor, and one that I let myself savor in the moment. I breathed a sigh of relief and found myself watching the scene as if I were out of my body, observing. And I was laughing. I had actually pulled it off, held it together. I sounded calm, practical, positive, certain. I almost believed it myself.

Until the next morning, as I was saying goodbye to my mom on the front porch. That morning, I lost it.

"I'm a-afraid," I sobbed, suddenly feeling like a five-year-old again, nose running and desperately needing my mom. And she was there, standing on the porch with me in her fuzzy, pale-green robe and slippers—all 5'4" of her—as brave and as fierce as any warrior going into battle.

"Look me in the eye," she commanded. "You have a choice about how you are going to handle this. Say, 'I'm going to be fine.' Say it!"

"I'm going to be f-fine," I blubbered.

"No," she shook her head hard. "Say it like you mean it."

"I'm g-going to be fine."

"Again. This time, like you believe it."

"I'm going to be fine." I was a little exasperated, but I tried. Because she's Mom, and I really wanted to believe it.

"Again."

I held my head up, squared my shoulders, and looked her straight in the eye. "I am going to be fine," I said slowly, deliberately, with what sounded like certainty. I surprised myself.

"OK," she nodded her head, satisfied. "Now write it down."

She opened the door and grabbed a pen and some paper off the bureau.

I wrote the words, my hand trembling.

In that moment, even when I felt like I was faking it, I put myself in the mindset of certainty. And I *felt* certain. Because, in that moment, I decided that I will NOT live in fear. I had tried on despair and anxiety for the first time in my life, and guess what?

I hated it.

I hated that pressure in my chest that caught me off guard and took my breath away.

I hated the racing heartbeat and the dizzy feeling that threatened to knock me off my feet.

Hated feeling weak.

Hated the terror and shock of knowing that, "I have cancer" was now my impossible yet undeniable reality.

Hated the relentless pounding of adrenaline through my veins as every cell in my body roared "*RUN!!!!*"

But how do you run from yourself?

In that moment, on that porch, I *decided* that, whatever my journey held for me, *I* am the one who gets to decide how I feel about it. I will not let fear grab the wheel and drive. *I'm* driving this bus.

I'm the one who decides what soundtrack plays in my head.

I'm the director of this movie.

Because, even though I can't control the situation, I *can* control how I respond. And right about now, that bit of control I had in a wildly uncontrollable situation gave me a sense of strength, a glimmer of peace. I am going to continue to *live* my life, wherever that journey takes me. Cancer does not define me. In fact, I'm not even going to call this cancer by its name. It doesn't even get a capital "C" anymore, either. It's been demoted to "c." It is not who I am. It's an experience I need to go through.

One week later, a letter arrived in the mail. In the envelope was another envelope marked *Susan, Warrior Princess*. And inside the envelope, in my slightly scribbly but nevertheless bold handwriting, was a scrap of paper with the words:

"I am going to be FINE."

I keep that note on a corkboard in front of my computer, to remind me of that decision.

I decide to feel optimism over despair.

I decide to be grateful instead of fearful.

I decide happy.

PS—In case you were wondering, the circumference of Tim's head IS perfectly normal, at 57 cm. The heads of the Denny clan weighed in at a generous 60 cm, including me!

2. Decide—Your Turn

"The Highway of Life is paved with flat squirrels who couldn't make a decision."

—John C. Maxwell

Happiness is a constant decision.

At any moment, life may conspire to throw something your way, and bam! You have a decision to make. How will you react? Are you going to let the weather or the news or someone else's crabby comment or post ruin your day? That decision I made on that front porch was not a one-time deal. I constantly have to remind myself of the ferocious certainty I felt that day so that I can keep making the choice over and over again.

This is why *deciding* to be happy is the first practice we have to master for more joy in life.

Every skill in this book is within your realm of doing. Right here, right now. Happiness is a set of learnable skills and a set of daily rituals, as much as it is a mindset. The Happiness Practices are the easy part. *Deciding* that you want to do the work, and committing to follow through? That's the hard part.

Our decisions shape our lives.

What is one decision you made that has dramatically changed your life for the better?

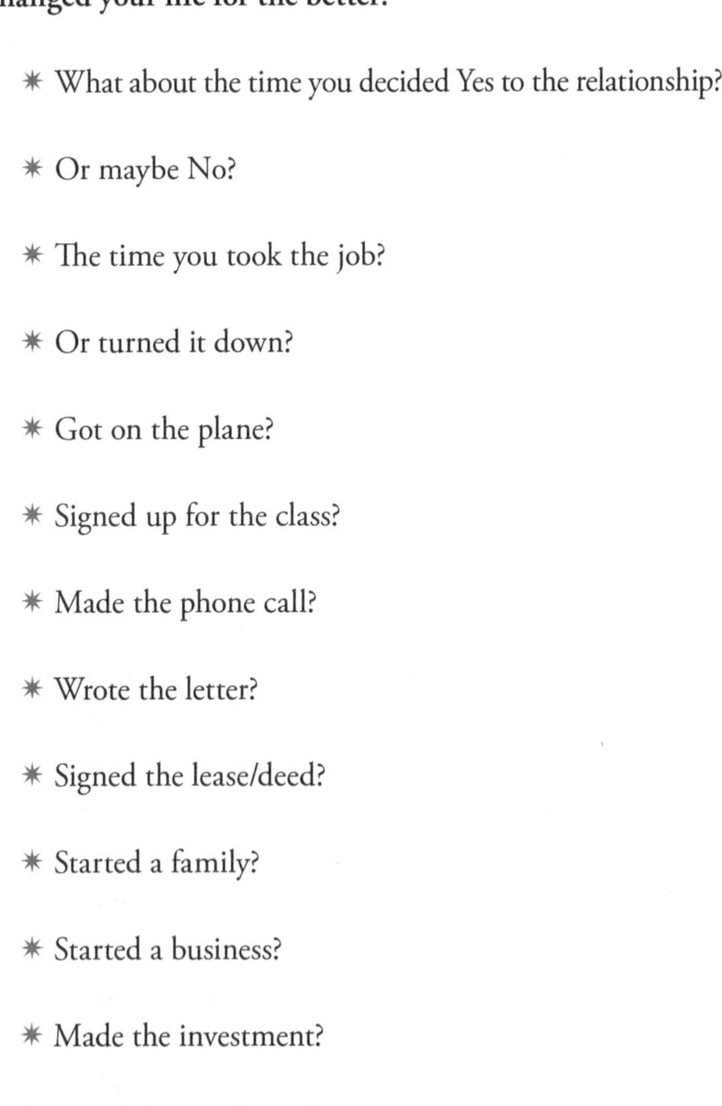

- What about the time you decided Yes to the relationship?
- Or maybe No?
- The time you took the job?
- Or turned it down?
- Got on the plane?
- Signed up for the class?
- Made the phone call?
- Wrote the letter?
- Signed the lease/deed?
- Started a family?
- Started a business?
- Made the investment?
- Hired the coach or the trainer?

Can you name one right now? Did it mean taking a risk?

When I look back at my life, the times I took a deep breath and made the decision to stretch myself—those were the moments that significantly shaped my life. The times I chickened out or waited too long to act and lost precious time—those decisions changed the course of my life as well. I can name those moments, and I regret them. What about you?

We talk a lot about deciding. But to truly *Decide*, we resolve, *we commit* to do something differently. The word "decide" comes from the combination of two Latin words:

1. *de* means "off"

2. *caedere* means "cut"

Or "To cut off," as in to cut off any other options or possibilities.

And that, my friend, is the tough part. Deciding means committing, and that requires risk.

Have you ever really wanted something but didn't follow through? Of course, you have. We all have. Maybe you wanted a better job, or to travel, quit smoking, lose weight. . . . Often, we don't truly decide because it's just too hard. We are afraid of loss, of cutting off other options. But playing it safe or keeping the status quo keeps us firmly in the "*Fine*" zone You know—not terrible, but not *Freakin' Awesome,* either. Just . . . *fine.*

It's far easier to complain, to be negative, to criticize, to settle. And, let's face it, sometimes it just feels good to whine. That's why most people aren't so happy.

The other evening, Tim and I were at a restaurant for dinner. I had skipped lunch to work and was now in full-blown "hangry" mode, grumbling over how long it was taking the server to acknowledge us and take our order.

Tim listened to me gretz for a while and then finally looked at me, eyebrow quirked, and asked, "Aren't you writing a book about happiness?"

"YES!" I snapped. "I KNOW what to do to feel happier right now—I just don't WANT to!"

It's a lot easier to blame other people or situations for making us angry or upset than it is to own up to the fact that we are *always, always, always* in charge of our emotions. It's *work* to have to accept responsibility for our own reactions.

What is an important decision you made that you've stuck with?

The times you've followed through on your decisions are the times when the pain of staying in your current situation was so intense, or the pull of moving to a different situation was so compelling, that you took action and stuck the landing. You'd had a strong reason, a strong WHY.

I have a good friend who has not been happy with her weight for most of her adult life. She wanted to lose the extra weight, of course, but just couldn't seem to commit to the hard, daily choices of drastically changing her diet and exercising differently. She's smart, beautiful, and accomplished, but one day she saw herself in a video and didn't recognize herself. *"I look like Jabba the Hut."* She had been a competitive swimmer in college and did not see this new shape as part of her athletic identity (more on the power of ***Identity*** in a bit.) So, she made a decision. A *real* decision.

> *"I don't want to be the fat aunt who stays on the sidelines. I want to have the energy to be active in my nieces' and nephews' lives."*

That's a pretty compelling WHY. She hired a trainer/nutritionist on the spot and committed to working out three times a week. She paid him in advance so she wouldn't back out so easily. Over time, she not only dropped the weight, but, because she had been cooking healthier foods, her whole family improved their health and energy levels. Plus she got a new wardrobe! And even better, she now has the energy to hike, and swim, and play tennis with her friends and family. Her nieces and nephews call her the "Cool Aunt."

> *"Once you make a decision, the universe conspires to make it happen."*
>
> —Ralph Waldo Emerson

Have you ever noticed how, once you *decide*—resolve to do something that is meaningful to you—the Universe rises up to meet you? If you decide and move forward with certainty, with intention, life meets you partway. There is a powerful momentum that comes with true decision-making.

For example, once I decided to write this book, within a week of mentioning it to friends, three people offered to put me in touch with published authors to learn from their experience.

The summer after I graduated from college, the friend who was planning to join me for two months of trekking across Europe backed out. I was determined to go. I ended up striking up a conversation with a girl in our apartment building's laundry room who, surprise, surprise, was looking for a travel companion for a summer adventure. That chance encounter, coupled with a real decision, led to a life experience and friendship I will always treasure.

My friend Janis was afraid to leave her secure corporate job and launch her own consulting business. She played it safe and dragged her feet for a few years, until the pull of her dream outpaced the comfortable drudgery of her current situation. The following week, she gave her notice and, during that *same* meeting, her boss asked her if she would be willing to take them on as a first client. The universe (along with a lot of hard work) subsequently delivered many clients that helped her build a successful business.

Everything starts with a decision—a decision to take action, a decision to shift a negative emotional state to a happier one.

Once I wrote down those words, **"I am going to be FINE,"** and decided to believe it and *act* on it, cancer didn't define or control me. It became an experience, an event in my journey. A chapter in my life, but nowhere near my Whole Story.

Happiness Practice

"Do or do not. There is no try."

—Yoda

What's one decision that will improve the level of happiness in your life? Or what's something going on in your life that you'd like to feel happier about? Maybe something you've been dragging your feet on? *Write this down!*

- Why is that important to you?
  -
  -
  -
  -

- What are the consequences of NOT following through on this decision? To you? To your loved ones?
  -
  -
  -
  -

- What do you stand to gain by following through?
  -
  -
  -
  -

* What's one action you can take *now* to put yourself on this course?
    •
    •
    •
    •

* How will making this decision make you feel?
    •
    •
    •
    •

3. Stack Life in Your Favor

"Live life like it's been rigged in your favor."

—Rumi

The day started out fine, and then, as days sometimes do, it took several unexpected turns. It began with a morning walk on a lovely spring day with Tim and the dogs.

Gunther, our fifteen-pound, fifteen-year-old Jack Russell rescue was especially peppy, walking jauntily with his ears and tail perked up and his little chest all puffed out. Tim stopped abruptly.

"What's in Gunther's mouth?"

Gunther's a shorty, and his mouth, along with the rest of him, is low to the ground. I crouched down to take a closer look. There were spindly, little dried-up twigs sticking out from underneath each side of his pointy nose. Then I looked closer. Those little dried-up twigs were not twigs.

"Aagghh—it's a dead bird!"

A very dead, very flat, very desiccated bird. And Gunther was not about to give it up without a fight. Luckily, we were across the street from a dog-loving neighbor and were able to hit them up for some treats. We managed to negotiate a trade with Gunther—the dead bird for a week's supply of liver snacks. There was no way he was dropping that prize for a standard-issue dog biscuit.

Crisis averted, we rushed back home late to find our electrician, Todd, parked outside of our house waiting for us. We quickly got him situated and, skipping breakfast (and coffee!), rushed upstairs to our virtual tax appointment. You do *not* want to be late for Arnold. He is excellent at accounting but has no patience and no sense of humor during tax season. Halfway into our call, which was running up dollar signs with each calculation, we heard the noise of a shop vac, followed by fast, heavy footsteps on the stairs.

"I'm so sorry," gasped Todd as he rounded the corner. "I hit a water pipe while fishing for a wire. But don't worry! I have a buddy who's a plumber, and he's on his way!"

He no sooner said this when Gunther, who had been curled up by my feet, sat up, looked straight at me, and promptly threw up all over the carpet. *Seriously?! Why can't it ever be on the kitchen floor?!*

A few hours later, exhausted, Tim and I collapsed onto the sofa. My thoughts were churning, my sugar levels were crashing from not eating, and I was on edge. Tim might have used a different word. I could feel the energy coming off of him as well.

Now, taken independently, each little inconvenience or frustration of the day was just that—an inconvenience or a frustration. But stacked on top of each other, the sum of those multiple challenges was quickly adding up to a "bad" day. I wanted to brush my teeth, go to bed, and call it a day. And it was only 2 p.m.

Sometimes, we don't even need life to surprise us with a stack. We do it to ourselves.

Does this sound familiar?

"Okay, I'm leaving for a business trip first thing tomorrow, so I need to pick up that blue jacket at the dry cleaner's, pack, get the project agreement to a client, write the document I promised, and pick up a birthday gift and/or bake cupcakes for school. Hmm, I think I can squeeze in a quick visit with my friends/parents/kids."

In the kingdom of **I Can Squeeze In One More Thing**, I am royalty. We live in an achievement-oriented, get 'er done culture, where we value the crazy-making behavior of packing in as many to-do's as we can. It's a sure-fire recipe for . . . well, crazy. Sometimes, something has to give. And that's okay. Give yourself permission to STOP THE CRAZY. If this is you, there are three magic words you can use to prevent that last straw from metaphorically breaking your back. Ready?

"No, thank you."

Try it now. Say the words out loud. Say it again.

See? You didn't faint. You haven't vaporized. You're okay.

Up until now, we've just been talking about everyday-problem stacking. There are times in life when multiple seemingly insurmountable problems stack up. Then it can feel like an avalanche. I spoke with a colleague recently and could tell from her tone of voice that she was having a tough day.

"You don't sound like yourself," I said. "What's going on?"

"I'm sorry," she sighed. "It's just that my mom's dementia is getting worse. And my dad is so stressed out and exhausted from taking care of her."

As if that weren't enough, her relationship with her fiancé was not going well, so she was thinking of moving back into her parents' basement, which was in the middle of being renovated, to help her parents. On top of all of this, she had a pinched nerve in her back and couldn't stand or walk without sharp, debilitating pain. Her go-to for managing stress was walking, and now even this wasn't an option.

"I just feel so overwhelmed," she lamented.

Well, of course. Who wouldn't feel that way? That's at least four or five big MTSTs *(Most Terrible and Stressful Things)* stacking up. Each one of those things by itself is difficult and complicated. Stack them on top of each other, and the burden must have felt unbearable.

Q: How do you dig yourself out of an avalanche?
A: One step, one action, one snowball at a time.

When I was going through **The Year That Shall Not Be Named**, I remember thinking *"Now I understand where the phrase 'One Step at a Time' comes from."* It was a struggle just to get through the day. Given the lack of control over everything that was happening, it helped to "**Unstack**" the heavy stuff by choosing one thing and taking action on that.

The thought of a long, multi-month recovery was overwhelming. Instead, I focused on one small action or two to chip away at the stack—doing my physical-therapy exercises for my shoulder, or reading just a few pages of a book, or taking ten minutes to go through emails. ***Progress!*** And progress builds momentum.

In the case of my co-worker, I did the one thing I could do—listened. I gently encouraged her to *unstack* by asking, *"If there is one thing you could begin to tackle, what might that be?"* She was feeling the most stress around her father being overwhelmed and came up with the brilliant thought to talk with her mom's case manager about getting some help for her and her dad. That's a great first step in chipping away at a very heavy stack.

Stack up the positives

Compared to my colleague's, my day was stacked with "champagne" problems. When this happens, it helps to vent a bit, sometimes with wine in hand, and then start piling on the positives. Because even in a day stacked with flattened-out birds, spewing water, tax bills, and dog vomit, there are good things to be stacked. We just have to notice them. Here's how my conversation went with Tim on the couch that afternoon:

"Well," Tim said, "it's painful, but the good news is that we have the money in savings to pay the tax bill."

I thought for a moment, knowing it was my turn. "Yes, and Gunther didn't actually *eat* the bird before he threw up on the carpet. That would have been *super* fun."

"Right—that bird met its maker long before it met Gunther. Plus, they were able to fix the water pipe without too much trouble."

"Uh, huh. And since we need to paint the ceiling anyway, why not just paint the living room, too?"

Tim chuckled at that one. "Nice try."

You get the picture. By saying, "No, thank you" to the extra, stressful thing, chipping away at the stack of tough stuff, and stacking up the positives, it's possible to catch our breath, shift our perspective, and maybe even feel a little happier. As always, it starts with a **decision.** We have to *want* to leave the Pity Party first in order to start unstacking and tackling the issues one at a time.

Sometimes we want to stack up the positives for more joy. Ric Elias, Tedx speaker and survivor of the Hudson River aircraft crash piloted by Captain "Sully" Sullenberger, talks about the concept of "*Three-fers.*"

A three-fer is a conscious stacking of three good things. If one good thing is good, two good things is better, then three good things is magical.

I love this concept.

For example, I've always felt that leisure travel—or any big, celebratory event—is an automatic three-fer:

You get the joy and fun of planning the event. One.

You get to enjoy the actual trip or celebration. Two.

Then, afterwards, you get to savor the photos and the memories. Bam! Three-fer.

Here's another:

1. For me, the pandemic inspired a weekly virtual Happy Hour with two of my very best friends, who live in different states. That's one, big, good thing right there.

2. During our Happy Hours, each of us is sure to wear one of our beautiful "Girlfriend Gifts"—a piece of jewelry or a scarf or sweater that we've given each other over the years. During lockdown, when we traded cute clothes and lipstick for yoga pants and lip balm, this felt positively dressed up and decadent. That's two.

3. And, my friend Linda bought us all lush, aromatic "Girlfriend candles." We light them during our calls so we can enjoy the fabulous scents while we laugh together and catch up. Bam! Three-fer.

And another:

1. My mom's health issues required regular visits to her cardiologist, which was an important but decidedly un-fun thing. She discovered that there was a cute little clothing shop near the hospital and would reward herself with a browse and sometimes a buy after her appointment. That's one.

2. Her friend Chris lived close by and would often join her so they could shop together. That's two.

3. And next to the cute little clothing shop, there was a bakery that made fresh coconut cake. Bam! Three-fer.

Let's say that it's a beautiful day but you have some work you need to finish after business hours.

1. What if you took your work with you and sat outside on the deck or patio? That's one.

2. Now, what if you brought a cold glass of fresh mint iced tea with you? That's two.

3. And what if you played some of your favorite music softly in the background? Bam! Three-fer.

or

1. Maybe you want to enjoy a walk through the woods or the park near your house. That's one.

2. And you take your dog with you, who has been cooped up all day while you worked and is thrilled at the prospect of going anywhere with you. Two.

3. And you pack some really great bread and cheese and a crisp apple to enjoy when you find a nice view. Bam! Three-fer.

Sometimes it's a stretch to get a three-fer, and that's okay. Even a two-fer makes a "just okay" or "not okay" experience much happier.

And it always helps to say *Bam!*

Happiness Practice

What's one thing you have coming up that you are not looking forward to? Perhaps a routine chore that has to be done?

* What's one thing you could do to make it a little happier?
    -
    -

* How might you make it a two-fer?
    -
    -

* A three-fer?
    -
    -

* What's one thing you have planned this week that you are looking forward to?
    -

* How could you make it a two-fer?
    -
    -

✷ A three-fer?

-
-
-

✷ Is there a Big Stack going on in your life right now? What's one thing you can do that's in your control to chip away at it?

-

✷ Who and what are your resources? How can they help you unstack?

-
-
-

✷ What can you say, "No, thank you" to?

-
-
-

4. Focus

"If you look the right way,
you can see that the whole world is a garden."
—Frances Hodgson Burnett,
The Secret Garden

A few years ago, I surprised my husband with tickets to see Derren Brown, a phenomenal illusionist who loves challenging his audience's perception of reality. I remember sitting in the theater, an aging beauty with plush, red velvet seats and gilded moldings, captivated by the performer on stage. At one point about midway through the show, Mr. Brown instructed the audience to "Keep your eye on the banana" which was displayed on a pedestal slightly left of center stage. For the next half hour, he performed amazing feats of magic. I don't remember all of the specifics, but I remember two things very clearly:

1. We were completely mesmerized.

2. All eyes were on the magician. We were so focused on his performance that we forgot about the banana.

Subsequently, we missed one of the funniest moments of the entire show.

During the show, as Mr. Brown performed on one corner of the stage, a very tall man wearing a gorilla suit walked on stage, paused, took the banana in his fuzzy paw, and calmly walked off stage. Almost no one noticed this, including me. How is it that 2500 people, looking directly at the stage and given specific instructions to "keep your eye on the banana" can miss a 6'4" man in a gorilla suit? Well, as this incredible entertainer knows, we were distracted, "misdirected" by something else, and missed the *real* show happening in the background.

This is more than just a fun memory.

It's a metaphor for how we go through much of our lives if we're not careful. Our lives are busy. At any moment, there is so much going on around us that we can allow ourselves to be misdirected and miss the One Thing that could be making us happier.

- We focus on something the boss said yesterday that irked us and don't notice the really funny observation our child, or partner, or friend just made.

- We focus on the jerk who cut us off in traffic and don't notice the gorgeous, technicolor sunset unfolding in front of us.

- We focus on the big project hanging over us at work and don't savor the delicious meal that someone took the time to make for us.

If I focused on it, I could spin you a real sob story.

* I could focus on the ten months that I experienced while recovering from complicated and painful vertebrae amputation surgery and, just four months later, complicated and painful surgery to repair the five fractures in my shoulder.

* I could focus on how I had to sleep sitting up to support my shoulder, with my weight on the exact, painful surgical site where I was newly missing my tailbone and a few others.

* I could let myself sink right back into those mornings, closing my eyes to the unwelcome light of the sunrise brightening up the living room where I slept upright in a hospital bed. Listening to the sounds upstairs of my family waking up—my husband's footsteps, the water running though the pipes with his morning shower.

* I could focus on how I dreaded those morning cues that signaled that soon I could no longer escape into sleep. I would have to drag myself out of bed and face the day with its new, foreign routine of cleaning tubes and drains and bandages, enduring painful therapy, and other constant reminders of what I had lost.

OR

* I could focus on another ten months of my recovery, with friends and loved ones stopping by daily to visit

with me, bringing soft blankets, fabulous books, and delicious food. Friends who sat with me or stood with me when I couldn't sit, somehow knowing just when to make me laugh and when I wanted to talk, or when to listen, or sit quietly beside my bed while we read our respective books together.

* I could focus on how the medical team on the neurosurgery ward cheered me on like an athlete the first time I walked a full lap around the floor. And how the physical-therapy team brought in chocolate cupcakes to celebrate my graduation to a home-therapy program.

* I could focus on the tender and funny way Tim would prop me up with pillows and tuck me in every night, and the gorgeous sunrises every morning, each a different work of art.

* I could focus on how Elsie, my greyhound, slept at the foot of the bed, pulling the comforter with her, resulting in a little game of tug of war that always made me smile.

* I could focus on these moments of joy and how lucky I was to live in a time and place where excellent healthcare was available to me. How lucky I was to have listened to the whispers of my body and sought out answers. How lucky I was that they found the tumor early and got it all.

* I could focus on how lucky I was to have a husband and family and friends who were there to care for me when I most needed them. How lucky I was to be so completely and unconditionally loved.

Now, which version of the story is true?

Both were.

Both versions describe the exact, same ten-month time period in my life. But the *decision* to intentionally focus on the more optimistic version of the story is what got me out of bed every morning, what gave me hope. This was the focus that I needed to pay attention to in order to do the things I needed to do daily to heal, get strong again, and move forward with my life.

Be careful where you put your focus. We give power to what we focus on.

Our brains are selective little buggers and are constantly making decisions, consciously and unconsciously, about what we focus on, what gets deleted, and what fades away into the background. My mom once said, "*I don't like to talk a lot about pain. I don't want to give it that much power.*" There is a whole lot of negativity around us, clamoring constantly for our attention. But there is also, at any given moment, so much grace, so much loveliness, so much light around us, if we only choose to see it. To focus on it. To celebrate it.

Try this:

Without looking around or concentrating too hard, close your eyes. With your eyes still closed, *remember*

everything that was in your line of sight. Then open your eyes again.

Right now, for me, it's my computer keyboard, because I'm awful about looking at my hands when I type, my journal, a couple of pens and pads of sticky notes, a stack of papers in slight disarray, the dark wood of my desk, and the wall behind me. Got it? Okay, GO!

Okay, now that your eyes are open again, and without moving your head—what ELSE do you see?

For me, it's all those things I saw before, *and* I see the corner of a lovely little oil painting of a snowfall in New England that a friend gave to me. If I look out of my periphery vision, I can see Elsie's feet straight up in the air as she sleeps on the window bench in my office. I see the corner of a note from a friend that I've kept for years since the diagnosis, reminding me that *I am Brave. I am Strong. I am Loved.* Wow, that focus just got a whole lot nicer, didn't it?

Andy Puddicombe, of Headspace fame, shares a metaphor on his meditation app that has helped me keep perspective during difficult times. "Life is sometimes filled with storm clouds. And sometimes, those clouds get so heavy and dark and foreboding that we feel overwhelmed. But remember, the blue sky is always there. We may not be able to see it at the moment, but it's always there for us, just above the clouds."

I love that image. It brings me peace focusing on the blue sky, knowing it is a constant—always there above the storm clouds, larger and more infinite than me, my circle, my world.

Here are two Happiness Practices that will help you **focus** on more joy:

1. Intentionally seek out what brings you happiness.

That may sound obvious, but happier people look for things to make them happy, even in life's shadowy valleys. For example, one of the characteristics that most attracted me to Tim is his love of fun. He is a professional magician himself (*I know—right?!*) and loves to surprise me. Sometimes that means concert tickets on a Tuesday. Sometimes that means a dozen fake eyeballs rolling on my pillow as I crawl into bed at night. It's a toss-up.

Years ago, he started a habit of looking for funny stories to share with me from his day.

- It could be the time Gunther, our Jack Russell mix, found an egg at the neighbor's Easter egg hunt. He has three teeth, and it took two people to wrestle it from him!

- It could be a bumper sticker on the car in front that read *"Where am I going? And what am I doing in this handbasket?!"*

- It could be the neighbor's six-year-old son, zipping down the sidewalk in his battery-operated red convertible, tree-shaped air freshener trailing off the back.

Funny things are *everywhere,* just like beauty, kindness, and grace are everywhere. We just have to notice them. By intentionally looking for these moments, we find more of them and can train our brains to focus more positively. Now, when Tim asks me for a funny moment *du jour* and I don't have one, I feel like a slacker for not paying better attention.

2. **Ask yourself better questions. And watch those dangerous "What if?" questions.**

Questions are one of the fastest ways to change your focus. We humans are amazingly creative people. When there is a vacuum of information, we can fill it with all kinds of scenarios. It's astounding how quickly our brains can go negative. One of the most potentially dangerous questions we can ask ourselves is *"What if?"*

"What if he/she doesn't return my call?"

"What if he doesn't get into that school?"

"What if the cancer comes back?"

"What if I lose my job?"

"What if she leaves me?"

"What if I can't pay the rent, mortgage, electric bill?"

If your brain goes to the "What if?" quickly re-focus to a better "What if?"—one that serves you.

For me, whenever my brain hits me with a "What if the cancer comes back?" *(usually around scan time)* I do my best to shake it off with a better question:

"What if I live to be a happy old lady of ninety-seven?"

"What if I used my experiences to help others in a meaningful way?"

"What am I going to do with this *next* half of my life?"

How was your pandemic? Covid was quite the test, wasn't it? It was devastating for many, and I am in no way minimizing the real toll it took on businesses, families, and lives. And yet, like other challenging times, it was not without its silver linings, if we choose to focus on them. I bet, if you think about it, you can truthfully answer both of these questions.

1. *What's one thing you missed due to Covid lockdown?*

2. *What's one thing that lockdown gave you that you wanted to keep or maintain after the pandemic was over?*

Think about that, and write it down now in your journal or in this book.

And try this:

The next time you're in a sticky situation, when your brain defaults to "This stinks!" try asking a better question. What if you intentionally asked:

What's good about this?

What brings me joy?

Who needs help today, and how can I help them?

Who do I miss that I can reach out to?

What am I grateful for? Oooh, this is a powerful one. So powerful there's a whole chapter on it . . .

Happiness Practice

Think of something that's bothering you or weighing heavy on your mind. What's the "What if?" that you are asking yourself? Write it down.

- What's a better "What if?" question? What's good about this? Write these down. Take your time. I'm not going anywhere.
  -
  -
  -
  -

- What *else* could be good about this? Write it down.
  -
  -
  -
  -

Practice using daily questions to focus your mindset:

- Start each morning asking yourself, "What am I grateful for today?"
  -
  -
  -
  -

Finish the day by asking, "What were three good things that happened today?"

-
-
-

✷ What made me happy? What brought me joy?

-
-
-

✷ What made me laugh today?

-
-
-

✷ Who do I love? Who loves me?

-
-
-

Write this all down!

"The only difference between a good day and a bad day is attitude."

—Dennis S. Brown

5. Choose Your People Wisely

"Surround yourself with only people who are going to lift you higher. The world is already filled with those who want to bring you down."

—Oprah Winfrey

I met my friend Charmaine when we were 16 years old, working at an ice-cream and sandwich shop in our hometown. We went to different high schools but bonded over boyfriends, butter-crunch ice cream, and the perils of scooping ice cream or frying up egg sandwiches in short, polyester skirts. She made me an ice-cream cone on my break that took her a full three minutes to scoop and weighed close to a pound—with extra chocolate sprinkles. That was the start of a lifelong friendship. We hung around so much together that my mom called her "My Brunette Daughter." And, just like a little sister, she still never fails to remind me that I'm the older one.

Over the years, we've shared life's journey in parallel. We know each other's hearts and heartaches. I know that she doesn't like revolving doors or her foods to touch each other on the plate. She knows why I celebrate like I won a scratch-off when I find a cute hat that fits and not to talk to me through the bathroom door.

I'm a good listener, and she's good in a crisis, a trait that served her well during her career with our city's police department and her rise to their Executive Protection Unit.

Charmaine is 90% *Vogue*, 10% biker chic. Okay, maybe 20%. She is striking, with dark hair, dark doe-eyes, and creamy skin. She's articulate, quick-witted, brave, fun, eminently rational—definitely a friend you want to have on your side.

But you do NOT want to mess with Charmaine. She is no shrinking violet.

One Thursday evening, Charmaine and I had plans to meet up with another friend for 2-for-1 lobster night at a popular local restaurant. We got there early, scored two seats at the bar, ordered drinks, and waited for our friend to arrive. As the crowd got busier, a young man—we'll call him Bud—elbowed his way through to the bar and, in a too-loud voice, barked out his order to the bartender.

You've met this guy. He does not do his gender any service.

As the Happy Hour went on, Bud got louder and more obnoxious, flicking lit matches at the bartenders for the sheer pleasure of provoking them. Finally, using the crowd as an excuse, he pushed his way uncomfortably into my personal space so that I slid off the bar stool. He immediately sat on it and claimed it as his own.

"Hey!" snapped Charmaine. "My friend was sitting there. Give her back her chair."

And Bud, seeing the *Vogue* and oblivious to the 20%, fired off the two words most likely to ignite a reaction in my otherwise level-headed friend:

"Make. Me."

The next moments were a blurry jumble. In the end, Bud was lying on his back on the floor, legs still wrapped possessively around the toppled bar stool, broken chunk of the bar counter gripped in both hands.

"Here!" Charmaine righted the barstool, and commanded me to sit, which I obediently, if self-consciously, did.

These are Your People.

I'm not suggesting Your People have to prove their love for you in a bar fight, although it could happen.

- But Your People stick up for you.
- Your People know your quirks and love you in spite of them—even *because* of them.
- Your People cheer you on through all of your milestones, small and big, from finding the hat that fits to walking out of that hospital ward.
- Your People unquestioningly believe in you and remind you of your best, strongest self when it's hard for even you to remember.
- Your People bring out your light and magnify it.
- And yes, Your People defend your honor and pull the chair out (metaphorically) from underneath the jerk who is bringing you down.

But what if you don't have People like this in your life right now?

Your People are out there, waiting for you. You just may not have met them yet.

Who would you like to have as one of Your People? Choose someone living their life at a higher level and then BE the kind of friend to them that you want. Be *Their* People. I don't think "friend-ing" is a word, but it should be. In fact, it should be a verb because the *act* of making friends requires just that: *action.* Friendships don't just appear. We are more connected than ever to our devices and social media with its cursory "likes" and superficial "friends." But finding someone in real life to connect with in a meaningful way takes *intention*. Friendships take time and nurturing and a series of actions and conversations. And making and maintaining friendships often takes courage.

When Tim started his magic career years ago, he reached out to several entertainers who were already successful in their business and shared his generous, "World of Abundance" mindset. He debated long and hard about doing this. "Why would they want to meet with me? I'm the new guy in their territory. I'm the competitor." But he took a deep breath and invited them all over for dinner and poker night. Four out of seven said, "Yes."

Can you imagine?

Five magicians playing poker every month with an accountant thrown in for good measure. (*The accountant cleaned up, by the way.)* It turns out that magicians, when they are not performing, spend a lot of time alone working on getting the next gig. And being a lone wolf can get kind of, well, lonely. These five magicians not only kept each other sharp with their collective knowledge and competitive ribbing, they became great friends. To this day, they help each other with shows and hold each other to a next-level standard that has set a high bar for entertainment in our entire metropolitan area.

My cousin Sandy has a neighbor who lives a few doors down from her. Over the years, they smiled at each other, waved "Hello," and then went about their days, as we do. One day, she learned that her neighbor's husband was very ill. So, Sandy decided to act. And Sandy (lucky for us) loves to cook.

Why make one course when you can make four?

And why make one, two, or three types of holiday cookies when you can make fifteen?

So, Sandy made her fabulous chicken pot pie and chocolate cake for her neighbor.

Three days later, as she was coming home from work, she almost tripped over the beautiful pot of spring flowers on her doorstep, a gesture of gratitude from her neighbor. Now, they stop and talk with each other when they see each other. If one is rushing off to work, to the grocery store, or to run an errand, they set a time to connect in the near future before they move on in their respective directions.

Find and surround yourself with people who want *your* best for you

"Who you spend time with is who you become," says Tony Robbins, and that has absolutely been my experience as well. I know from the research in my field of professional Learning and Development, that the number-one influence on employees' behavior and performance on the job is *not* our level of compensation. In many cases, it's not even our manager.

It's our *peers.*

Our peers hold us to a collective standard—whether that's high or low, or anywhere in between. How often have you heard of the "good" kid, hanging out with the wrong crowd, who demonstrates less-than-desirable behaviors? On the other hand, think of the teams you've been part of, the coaches you've met throughout your life, the social circles you move in.

Haven't you had people in your life who have challenged you to raise yourself to a higher standard?

It is critical to our happiness to make conscious choices about who we spend time with.

- If you want a strong relationship with your significant other, it helps to hang out with other couples who are in solid, happy relationships.

- If you want to contribute and give back to others in a bigger way, spend time with people who have philanthropic, generous-minded spirits.

- If you want to practice your craft—whether it's music, dance, sports, art, or technology—then surround yourself with people who are doing the same and who encourage you to grow and aspire to your best in this area.

Who do you know and love and/or respect who holds you to your higher standard?

Note, and this is important, that it's *your* higher standard they hold you to, not theirs. The absolute best mentors and coaches I've worked with over the decades have a knack for seeing the potential of their team members and hold them to achieving it. "I've seen you do this, and I know you're up to the task." "You have it in you. You just don't see it yet, but I do." Your People believe the best in you and want you to be that even-better version of *you.*

Who's on your personal BOA?

Many companies have a **Board of Advisors**, a group of thoughtfully chosen individuals who provide objective counsel and support to help the business owner achieve his or her goals.

Why not form your own personal Board of Advisors?

These are the people in your life who support you in living your best life. When I have a difficult decision to make, I picture myself at the head of a long table in a boardroom (albeit in some tropical, open-air locale), surrounded by My People. I ask myself, *"How would they advise me in this situation*?" I have living BOA members to whom I can reach out directly. But some of my BOA members are no longer on this Earth. The example they set while they lived, however, still shapes who I am, and strive to be, today. I can hear their voices, and I know their counsel. How about you?

My Board is fluid, with members changing, depending upon the situation or problem that I'm working to resolve. At the moment, here's who is sitting on my Writer's Board:

- Tim, sitting directly to my right, who makes me laugh, and reminds me to always look for magic and wonder in the world.

- Bob, my friend and mentor in business and life, who taught me the elegant power of sincere, well-told stories and how great leaders lead from behind and put their people front and center.

- My friends and fellow authors who provide feedback with ruthless compassion, and somehow manage to strike a delicate balance of encouragement while wielding a samurai sword of "cut the crap."

- My mother, whose voice tells me (often quite loudly) to "Step it up!" and gives me a standing ovation when I do.

- I always have a child on my Board, to remind me to see the world with fresh eyes, from a creative, unbridled perspective. This time it's Hannah, my neighbor's seven-year-old, who loves strawberries, her baby sister, bugs that land in her hands, and anything pink.

- There are also a number of well-known speakers and coaches whom I've never met in person but who are a consistent source of inspiration and focus in my ear while I'm on the treadmill, walking the dogs, or waiting at stoplights on commutes. Who says you have to know your BOA personally? It's **Your** Board.

It's a very long table. I know how lucky I am.

Don't waste time with the energy drainers

Who are the people who bring out the best in you? Are there others who make you feel like you're walking on eggshells? Perhaps you have a friend who is a "taker." You find yourself giving and giving, but they never seem to reciprocate. I'm not suggesting friendships are *quid pro quo*: "*You do that for me and I'll do this for you.*" Your People don't keep score. They don't have to, because you both do things for each other out of love, knowing it will all be better than fair in the end.

- But maybe they are critical or judgy about you or others, and you find yourself a little drained, a little diminished, whenever you talk.

- Or maybe they consistently obsess over everything that could possibly go wrong, or all of their troubles, or the world's troubles.

- Or maybe they drone on with that constant buzz of, "Ain't it awful?"

It's easy to talk about the negative.

According to the National Science Foundation, an average person has about 12,000 to 60,000 thoughts per day. Of those, 80% are *negative.*

But you are SO far above average.

Do you really want to waste your time with that kind of oppressive negativity? When you hear it from the people you love, nip it fast. Once again, it's a *decision.* We all have our moments. Sometimes we have many moments strung together over many days. But if you are experiencing a pattern of negativity that has escalated to a level that concerns you, then perhaps you can choose to steer the conversation in another direction or limit your time together. Better yet, you can make the brave choice to call out that behavior and ask for their help in focusing more positively.

You can't fight crazy. If this person is truly toxic, run in the opposite direction as fast as you can. However you address it, be aware of the energy drainers, and don't let yourself get sucked in. It will douse your spark and siphon off your happiness.

Joy is magnified through our relationships with Our People.

When we are with Our People, we both thrive from these shared experiences, and, somehow, together, we become more than we were before.

It's been said that people come into our lives for a reason, a season, or a lifetime. For however long they are with you, take the time to *find, nurture*, and *act* for Your People. They will be there for you, to support you through the tough times, and celebrate you from wherever they are.

Happiness Practice

* Who are Your People? Who do you know and love and/or respect who believes in you?
  -
  -
  -
  -
  -

* What can you do or say to thank them and continue to strengthen that relationship?
  -
  -
  -
  -
  -

* Who would you like to have on your Board of Advisors? What is it about this person that you appreciate?
  -
  -
  -
  -
  -

✷ Where will they sit? How will they support and advise you in life?

-
-
-
-
-

✷ Is there someone in your life who is draining your batteries? Assuming you want to maintain this relationship, what can you do or say to minimize the negativity?

-
-
-
-
-

Are you writing this down?

"Stay close to people who feel like sunlight."

—Xan Oku

6. Clean Up Your Mess

"Be Considerate and Clean up After Yourself."

—Instructions for the washroom.

And for Life.

I adore my brothers.

On my short list of "people I would do anything for and travel far to spend time with," they are at the top of the list.

But that wasn't always the case.

Growing up, we had some epic kid-battles. A scrawny, towheaded girl of eight, I was no match for my big brother, John, who, at age 10, had the brawn of a middle-school wrestler. When we dug into each other's first or last nerves, which was frequently, my strategy was "Scratch, Run, and Lock." Specifically, I'd hit 'em hard with the fingernails, race up the stairs to the one bathroom in our house as fast as my skinny legs could carry me, and frantically scramble with the lock on the door before he could come barreling through.

I had perfected it.

If, on an off-day, I stumbled on the stairs or fumbled with the bathroom door lock, the WaterPik Vs. Water Cup battle, hair pulling, and bloody-murder hollering that ensued were sure to send Mom flying up the stairs after us. This inevitably ended with more yelling: "**You kids knock it off! Now!**" and each of us being sent to our respective rooms.

Of course, the only person who could so much as threaten to lay a hand (or WaterPik) on me was John. Look out, Jimmy Litzko or any other little neighborhood bully who picked on me. I have a very vivid memory of John stalking up the hill to the Litzko house, fists clenched at his sides, retribution in his eyes. He never even had to step foot on their lawn. Poor little Jimmy melted down like a four-year-old, shouting through the screened window, "I'm sorry! I'm sorry! I'll never ever call her a frog face again!"

Yep, Jimmy totally had a crush on me.

In high school, John and I did our separate thing. He played sports, dominated ping pong and basketball tournaments, and occasionally skipped class to set fire to a mattress or two. I sang in an acapella traveling chorus, edited the school's newspaper, and occasionally missed curfew to give heartburn to a parent or two.

John and I no longer fought in hand-to-nails combat, of course. There was the standard sibling rivalry. But we got along okay at the family dinner table and on camping vacations. In fact, there wasn't one specific moment or rift that I can put my finger on. Over time, we just kind of grew . . . apart.

Good relationships take time and attention (See **Choose Your People Wisely**), and John and I didn't give each other a whole lot of either during those years. The funny thing about a little divide is that it can quickly grow into a chasm if we aren't careful, if we don't pay attention. We went about the business of living our separate lives as if that were the normal course of our relationship, a *fait accompli*, just the way things were. Indifference became our habit.

And then came the day that I woke up for the first time in my life as *Aunt* Susan.

John and Anne had had a baby boy, Ryan Jack. He was the first baby in our family, named after my father. Here was this beautiful new little soul in the world, who shared our family DNA and already, the unmistakable baby-sized version of the Denny head, along with the promise of John's oversized hands. Yesterday, we were a family of seven, and now we were eight. *How amazing is that?!* My heart swelled with love for this new little being, the result of the love of countless generations before us, a harbinger of infinite possibilities that lay ahead.

The first time I met my new nephew, I saw my brother John—I mean *truly* saw him—for the first time in a long time. I marveled at his frequent laugh, which came so spontaneously now, and admired the easy-going, cocktail-umbrella-drink loving, snort-through-your-nose funny, softhearted, gentle giant of a man he had become. *When had this transformation happened? How had I missed all of this?*

And that's when I realized: I was a foreigner in my brother's life.

The hundred and fifty miles that separated me from my brother and his family may as well have been ten thousand. I had a Dickens-esque moment, seeing toddler Ryan crying and pulling away from me, the Strange Aunt, whom he saw just a handful of times a year. In a blink, I saw him in elementary school, coerced by his mom to write Thank You notes for the twice-a-year gifts exchanged awkwardly at family holidays. I realized, with a deep stab of regret, that I had let my relationship with my brother erode to the point where I was now alienated, on the outside fringes, watching his new family like a sentimental visitor staring through a plate-glass window. I was not *in* the scene. That broke my heart.

So, I *decided* then that I needed to change my relationship with John. And to do that, *I* needed to change.

Knowing the infinite power of words, and ambivalent about my ability to initiate a heart-to-heart without screwing it up, I sat down with a pad of notebook paper and my favorite pen and poured my heart out into a letter. I wrote, and re-wrote, and re-wrote again until I was certain that there was not one, tiny, minuscule fraction of an inkling of blame in any of the sentences—or in any of the lines between them. The stakes were painfully high. This letter was a pure-hearted appeal, a vulnerable and open love letter to my family, to my future.

Here are the four elements of that life-changing letter:

1. **No Blame.** I owned my part in the fractures of our relationship. There was no "*You did this to me.*" There was no "*You made me feel this way . . .*" See how that puts you on the defensive?

2. **Instead, I shared my feelings**, how important he and his family were to me, and the loss I felt at not being more involved in his life.

3. **I shared the vision of how I wanted our relationship to be,** the kind of aunt I wanted to be to Ryan, and sister to him and to Anne.

4. **Finally, and this is IMPORTANT: I made sure that it was okay for my brother to ignore The Letter.** Yep, he did not need to even acknowledge this genuine, heart-on-my-sleeve letter. He had a free pass. He was off the hook. I very intentionally wrote these exact words: "*Unless you want to, you never even need to acknowledge that you received this letter. And I'll never bring it up.*" I was not going to put pressure on him to feel obligated to feel or do anything differently. I wanted him to know that he was important to me and that I was going to work on our relationship, spend time with him and his family, and enjoy getting to know him and who he was now. Not just as my brother, but as my friend.

So, what was his reaction to The Letter?

Truthfully? I have no idea. In fact, to this day, I don't know if John even received that letter, let alone what he thought of it. Because, as promised, I never brought up. And he never mentioned it.

And it doesn't matter.

Here's what matters:
Because I changed, so did our relationship.

I started making an effort. I made the six-hour round-trip drive every four to six weeks to visit. I called and, later, texted and emailed. We discovered we enjoyed each other's company and began making plans and arranging our schedules to include each other. We met halfway for lunch, or at Ryan's T-ball—then baseball—games, and for cookouts afterwards. And at some point, surprisingly early on in this new relationship, John changed, too. We both decided to reach out, to include each other. Today, we are very much *in* each other's lives. He is one of my favorite human beings on this planet, and I cannot imagine my life without him and his, and my, family.

Pop Quiz: **How many people does it take to change a relationship?** I used to think it took two, but I'm not so sure anymore. It takes two to actively *be* in the relationship, to nurture and maintain it. But sometimes it can take just one really determined person who is willing to take the first step to change it. And maybe even the second step, and a third, and a fourth. . . .

Our friend Dave came from a long line of family estrangements.

His dad no longer talked with his mom.

His uncle no longer talked with his daughter.

His aunt no longer talked with her sister.

And his sister no longer talked with anybody.

What caused these falling-outs? Well, like most separations, Dave can trace them all back to hurt, anger, pride, rejection, even open antagonism. But, as Dave looks back, the fractures often had their roots in indifference and apathy.

"Our family never ate dinner together every night like most families. We had nothing in common. In fact," he joked *(sort of)*, "my parents had their own His and Hers side of the kitchen refrigerator."

So, when Dave's dad, as they were cleaning up the dishes from his 50th wedding-anniversary celebration, abruptly announced that he would be leaving his wife and moving in with another woman he had been secretly bowling and sleeping with for the past four years, what do you think Dave's response was?

Well, for years afterwards, they were estranged. Dave didn't talk with his dad or accept any communications from him. He'd walk out of the room if anyone so much as mentioned his dad's name. And . . . he went on with the days of his own life, vowing to never become his dad.

Then came the phone call that informed Dave that his father's growing forgetfulness had slipped cruelly into full-blown Alzheimer's.

"I forgave him, got on a plane, and flew down to see him."

"Whoa, whoa, whoa—hold on a minute! You hadn't talked with your dad for years," I pressed, "then you just decide to up and forgive him and get on a plane to visit him? Why? And why *now*?"

"Because I knew he didn't have much time. And I had no choice." (*Except we all know that he did.*)

"What I mean is, I couldn't have *lived* with my choice. I didn't want another broken-family chapter in my life history."

There is so much I love about Dave's story:

* How a **decision**—made in a flash of a moment, and the action he subsequently took, completely changed the story.

* How the **focus** on what "could be" overcame the "what was."

- How the **meaning** he took from his relationship with his dad and the family he came from impacted the intentional way he nurtures and loves the family he created as an adult.

Because if you met Dave, with his easy grin and infectious, exuberant laugh, poking fun at himself and wearing his heart on his sleeve, you would know instantly that he broke the family cycle of secrets and psychological punishment. We joke that Dave's blood type is B+. It's well-earned, because he works very hard to *be positive*. And he is never happier than when he is with, talking about, or even thinking about his own beloved wife and family.

"You can't have happiness without love," he reasons.

"It's not a person's mistakes which define them—
it's the way they make amends."
—Freya North

These are examples of big, relationship-rending messes. But what about those little ones that unexpectedly pop their ugly heads up all too regularly?

My friend Mia recounted how she and her close friend Val were driving home from the airport after a trip to New York City, where they had enjoyed a fabulous week of theater, shopping, and restaurants. Val, behind the wheel, tossed Mia her phone and said, "I'm really low on gas. Find me a station?" Mia, unfamiliar with Val's phone, fumbled for several minutes before Val, impatient and stressed with the traffic, snapped, "You're a F-ing IDIOT!"

Only she didn't say "F"-ing.

Time slammed to a halt.

"What happened?" I asked, aghast. Mia hesitated, her face clouding with the memory. "We both waited a minute," she said. "Then she apologized. She said she didn't mean it, and I believed her. But it felt like she had punched me in the stomach."

"What did you do?" I asked, feeling such a stab of pain for my friend that I felt like the one being emotionally gut-punched.

"I gave her the benefit of the doubt. I decided not to take it personally."

Now, Mia is one of the most gracious, elegant, intelligent women I know. This woman leads teams of other teams of leaders at a fast-growing tech firm. Not only is she the polar antonym of a "f-ing idiot," if anyone can take the high road and give a more positive **meaning** to a challenging event, she can. Except that this event happened several years ago. And it still bothers her.

What to do?

Mia decided to forgive her friend and let it go. She chalked the outburst up to a lot of Big Stress stacking up on Val, including the recent loss of her father and her daughter's substance-abuse problems, all blanketed in a nice, thick layer of jet lag with a traffic-jam cherry on top. If, however, that breach continues to bother her or threatens to damage their friendship, then she might choose to address it directly. Yes, even years later.

The happiest relationships are built on a careful balance of letting the small stuff roll off our shoulders, while directly addressing the stuff that *really* bugs us.

While there are entire books written about communications in relationships, there are a few no-fail practices that I've picked up over my years of helping others manage conflict and build trust. And when I decide to actually ***Do*** the stuff I ***Know*** and teach other people, using these skills has infinitely impacted the quality of happiness in all of my relationships.

Ready?

1. **Slay the dragon when it's small.**

Those little hurts quickly fester and grow, and soon that carelessly tossed comment has morphed into a monster that would make even a paleontologist shudder. Don't wait for those little dragon-ettes to grow teeth and scales and power. The bigger they are, the more emotional *we* are, the harder they are to slay. It's a lot easier to stomp on a gecko than it is to slay a T-Rex. (*Reptile metaphor aside, I would never intentionally stomp on a gecko. You know that, right?)*

You get the point: Nip the problem while it's still small by addressing it as soon as possible. Take a deep breath, square your shoulders, and deal with it NOW. (Read **Stand Up Straight.**)

2. **Ditch the Blame Game**

A great way to begin this courageous little dragon-slaying conversation is with four Magic Words: "I need your help."

When someone confronts you with a "*You* did this. . . ." or "*You* make me feel. . . ." how does that make you feel? Defensive, right?

Whereas, when someone you truly care about asks for your help, I'll bet you'll climb all kinds of mountains to be there for them. That's the kind of person you are.

Using "I" words instead of "you" helps to neutralize tension so you can carry on and have an actual adult conversation. When you use "I," you own the feelings, as in "I felt . . . upset when this happened." And no one can argue how you feel.

3. Apologize. Forgive. Repeat.

When you realize you've made a mistake,
take immediate steps to correct it.
—Dalai Lama

Do you need to apologize to someone?

Then make it a real, heartfelt apology. We can all smell those fake-o ones a mile away:

"I'm sorry if . . . you feel that way."

"I'm sorry, but. . . . you started it."

These are not real apologies. Eliminate the "ifs" and "buts." They minimize the apology and deflect blame—not the best recipe for building trust in your relationships.

There are all kinds of ways to apologize well, but the keys are to:

* **Check your intent**

  Are you truly sorry? Or are you *sorta kinda* sorry but are also cool with shifting the blame so you still get to be right?

  Are you minimizing your part in the problem or justifying your bad behavior? To truly apologize well, we need to be okay with being vulnerable and admitting we blew it. You are making *your* apology; this is not about pointing out *their* faults. Re-read "Ditch the Blame Game" above. Read it one more time.

  Look them in the eye and say the words "I'm sorry." Not "I'm sorry, but.." No buts! Our brains automatically delete everything before the "but" and focus only on what comes after it.

  "I'm sorry" carries more weight than "Sorry." Just like *"I* love you" carries more weight than "Love you." It just does.

* **Own up to the mistake**—it's important that the other person knows that you understand what you did that you're sorry for. Then empathize with how that behavior may have hurt them. "It was rude of me to interrupt you like that. That must have felt like I didn't appreciate what you were saying. What you say IS important to me. There was no excuse for interrupting."

* **Ask for forgiveness**—"I hope you can forgive me."

* **Ask "Are we okay?"** Then listen and be prepared to discuss further if they need to.

4. Forgive

It takes a strong-hearted person to apologize. And it takes an equally strong-hearted person to forgive. This second part of the process—forgiving—is just as important as the apology.

Because if we don't forgive, if pride or the-all-too-human instinct to push back takes over, those ugly relationship dragons grow like Godzilla on prednisone.

Sometimes we need a cooling-off period. When we are emotionally charged, it sometimes helps to say, "I really want to have this conversation with you, but I need a breather first." Take a breath. Go for a walk. Going for a walk together is very powerful in terms of reconciliation. If it's important, it's worth taking the time to take a breath and *then* talk it out. But don't wait too long.

What if it's too late to make amends?

My colleague Sandra grew up with a father who was emotionally abusive. For years, she harbored anger and resentment toward him. When he died of lung cancer, she was not there. There were no dramatic bedside apologies or confessions, no forgiveness, no closure. Nothing.

The other day she mentioned that it was her father's birthday, and she was going to put flowers on his grave. I looked up, surprised.

"My dad never apologized when he was living. There's no way that he can apologize now that he's dead," she explained. "But I realized *I* was the one who was suffering. I got tired of being angry. The only way to control my own happiness and well-being for the rest of my life was to forgive him. And I don't need an apology from him to do that."

That's powerful stuff. We don't need an apology to forgive someone, even if they are no longer here.

It's never too late. Good relationships take time and attention. *Make* the time and give attention to these small and large rifts that crop up. You're worth it, and so are the people you love.

You can't have happiness without love.

Happiness Practice

1. Is there someone you need to apologize to?
    -
    -
    -
    -
    -

2. Why is it important for you to apologize?
    -
    -
    -
    -
    -

3. What might it cost you to apologize? What might it cost you if you do *not* apologize?
    -
    -
    -
    -
    -

4. How and when will you do this? Would it help to write a letter?
   -
   -
   -
   -
   -

5. Who do you need to forgive?
   -
   -
   -
   -
   -

6. Why is it important for you to forgive them? How and when will you do this?
   -
   -
   -
   -
   -

7. Be Gentle with Yourself

"Promise me you'll always remember
that you are braver than you believe,
stronger than you seem,
and smarter than you think."
—Winnie the Pooh

One of my happy places is my Saturday-morning painting class. A dozen of us put aside our errands and to-do's for a few hours to drink coffee, catch up on each other's lives, and paint. One day, as I contemplated how strange noses look up close, I heard Jane mumbling to herself from behind her canvas.

"Oh, this is awful. This is terrible! I've just wrecked 40 hours of work." She continued to grumble, her voice charged and critical. I set my brush down and walked around to look at this "travesty" sitting on her easel.

It was stunning, of course.

In front of me was a beautiful New England harbor scene, with the sunrise colors spreading out over the water. I could practically hear the fishermen as they pulled in their haul and swatted each other's backs, celebrating their bounty. The seagulls hovering nearby looked like they would fly from the canvas as they darted at the fish spilling over the boat's deck.

"What are you talking about, Jane?" I asked. "You've captured the colors, the mood, the *aliveness* of the moment beautifully!"

"No," she said, shaking her head definitively. "I'm going to throw this away and start over."

My fellow painters quickly chimed in. For the next few minutes, we alternately encouraged her *and* threatened to throw ourselves bodily between her and the trash can. Finally, she promised she would step away from the painting, take a deep breath, and come back to finish the scene another day.

Why is the loudest voice in our head often that D#*n Inner Critic?

Jane was about to scrap a beautiful work of art, all because of that nasty voice in her head. The Inner Critic shackles us with doubt, thwarts our courage, and steals our joy. Think of how many things we don't do, or throw away, because that inner critic says, "It's not good enough."

Let's revisit *Decide Happy's* definition of happiness:

The world needs us to be our most ***loving, calm, moving-forward, contributing best.*** We can't possibly experience happiness, live life to the fullest, and contribute our best if we are berating ourselves and whittling away at our own sense of self-esteem.

The best way to silence the critic?

1. **Quit allowing it so much air time.**
   - Remind yourself who's the boss of you—*YOU!* There's a post-it note on the laptop I use to write that reads, "Silence the Inner Critic, and trust that it will flow." It's right above the one that says, "Just F-ING WRITE!!!"

2. **Redirect the critic with a better question.**
   - Instead of saying, "I can't," ask "What if . . . ?"
   - Instead of "It won't work," ask yourself, *"How* can I make this work?"

Later that same day, I met my friend Luisa for lunch. She was **stacking** up a doozy of a pile of stress. In addition to managing her mother's living situation from a thousand miles away and working full time in a new job, she was also hosting a graduation party for her son the following week. Luisa is an amazing cook, and is known for her traditional *biscoitos* butter cookies, a generations-old recipe passed down to her from her great-great-grandmother. She had decided that this graduation party could be successful *only* if she personally mixed, rolled, shaped, baked, iced, and boxed 300 handmade Portuguese pastries.

"I can't get it all done," she said miserably, her eye pinched shut with the thought. "I feel like such a failure."

I wanted to reach across the table and flick her forehead.

I curbed myself (barely) and asked, "What are the consequences to this party if you *don't* make the cookies? And what are the consequences to *you* if you do?"

"Well," she sighed. "The party will go on regardless, of course. But I will be a stressed-out, sleepless mess if I try to tackle all that baking."

Exactly.

She ended up making one batch of the pastries for her son and visiting mother. The rest of us had to rough it with a catered feast that included half a dozen varieties of mouth-watering pastries, cakes, and other assorted delicacies.

Why do we set such arbitrary standards that can only stress us out and sap our joy?

And who sets these standards?

Do you?

Or are you letting other people dictate what self-worth looks like for you?

Maybe people you don't even know well or like very much?

Social media only heightens the self-perception that we're "not good enough." We see the accolades, adventures, and milestones on social media and think, "Wow! I thought I was doing okay but, compared to what I see Amanda, and Jim, and Chris doing—I'm a real slacker!"

But what we are really seeing is an illusion.

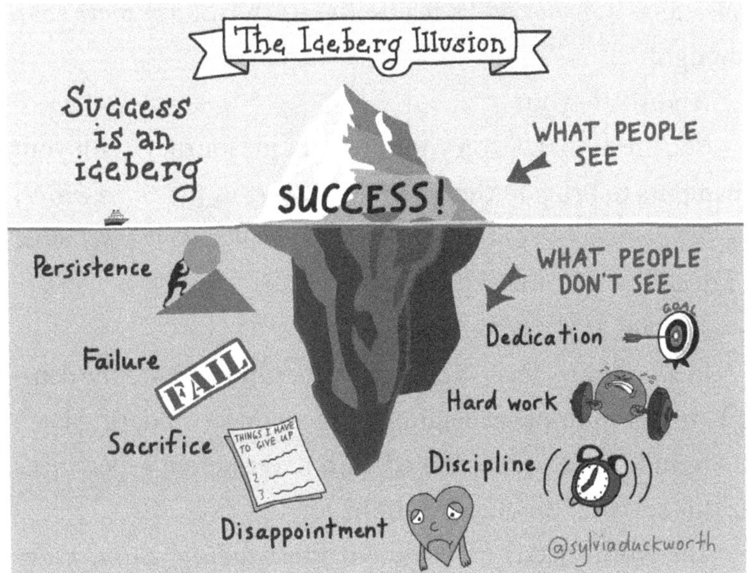

http://sylviaduckworth.com

How often do we hear about the pop star or entrepreneur who is heralded as an "overnight" success, only to learn that they slugged through years of rejection, criticism, and hard work to achieve their goal? We see the culmination of years of hard work and experience, but not the sacrifice, frustration, and plain old hard work leading up to it.

Comparing yourself to others who appear to have it all is an HOV lane to unhappiness.

I see the published author with three best-selling books, a TED talk with nine million hits and think, *"Who am I to think I can do this? I could never do that. I'm not good enough, young enough, experienced enough, connected enough.. . . ."*

And then I stop, challenge that thought, and ask a better question: *Why not me?* Because the truth is, I am *more* than enough.

And so are you.

You are a miracle, on your own unique journey, with your own gifts to bring to the world. Who else, in the *entire history of humankind*, has *your* story, your personality, your *exact* series of decisions and life experiences?

No one, that's who. Only you.

In all of time, there is only one you. Only you are the compilation of multiple generations of genetic lottos dating back thousands of years, combined with never-before experiences at this specific, unique time in history.

The world needs us to be our most ***loving, calm, moving-forward, contributing best.***

The world needs us to stop second-guessing ourselves and let our light shine.

When I'm being critical of myself, it helps me to remember the words of my friend, Susie Rinehart. Susie is a respected leader, author, mom, and champion ultra runner. *Because, why run 26 miles when you can run 50+?* She is also a reformed perfectionist. Despite all of her accomplishments, Susie still felt anxious and hollow, like she was "chasing worthiness."

One day, doctors discovered a tumor on her brainstem that threatened everything. For Susie, cancer was a wake-up call. She realized she had been silencing her voice out of fear of being "less than" perfect. So, she decided she would live life differently and keep the promise she made to herself: "I choose joy over fear. I choose *brave over perfect*." As a result, she is thriving in her own life and making a massive positive difference in the lives of so many others.

- Are you hesitating about something important out of fear of being less than perfect?
- What if you took imperfect action and erred on the side of *brave* over *perfect*?
- What if you took a leap of faith for *progress* over *perfect*?

We all have strengths and weaknesses. How is it that we often focus on our weaknesses and minimize our strengths? We have it all backwards.

Shore up your weaknesses.
But obsess over your strengths.

None of us can be good at everything. But each of us can be great at a few, highly impactful things.

Try this:

1. Think of a person in your life who has had a positive impact on you. Got it?
2. What are one or two of this person's strengths? *(Quickly—don't overthink this!)*

Maybe they are honest, kind, funny, perceptive, empathetic. Maybe they are practical, or analytical, or enthusiastic. Whatever it is, I bet their strengths came to you pretty quickly. Of course, this person has weaknesses, too. But they've still had a hugely positive impact on you, *despite* their weaknesses.

One of the advantages of working in the field of professional training and coaching is that I've had every skill and talent test imaginable. As a result, I'm crystal clear on my strengths and weaknesses. I sometimes still struggle with control issues. Also, I'm visionary, not a systems-thinker.

On the other hand, I know *to my core* that I'm good at:

- Communicating and building relationships.
- Creative thinking and problem-solving.
- Seeing the best in others and helping them tap into their strengths, even when they don't see it for themselves.

But you don't need formal assessments to identify your strengths. You already have the resources: *Your People.*

6-3-3

Here's a simple but effective tool to help you identify and focus on your strengths. I call it "6-3-3."

- **6**—identify at least six people whose opinion you value.
- **3**—Ask each of them to share three descriptions of your strengths with you.

* **3**—Review the compiled lists you get back from everyone, and then look for three similar descriptions. Three similar descriptions or words is a pattern. You may see one pattern, or you may see two or three. Take note: every pattern equals one of your strengths.

Let me give you an example of how this works:

First, here is the note I sent to My People, asking them for help with my 6-3-3:

Subject Line: I need your help, please!

Hello Dear Friend,

I need your help with a little project I'm working on—me!
Can you think of three descriptions that capture my ***strength of character****?*
Choose what comes to mind first. Keep it real!

Love,
Susan

Then, sit back, and let the love roll in. The descriptions Your People share with you will not only leave you feeling like the Rock Star that you are, but also, you'll be amazed at the patterns you will begin to see. Your People may use different words, but look for similarities. The picture will begin to crystallize.

Here are some of the responses I received, roughly grouped into similar categories/patterns:

* Listening
* Make those around you feel comfortable
* Definitely empathetic
* You listen without judging
* Empathetic
* Regarding others—put yourself in the shoes of those you are with
* Compassion and kindness
* My go-to on a really bad day

* Resilient
* Persevering
* Determined
* You handle obstacles
* Strong
* Tenacious
* Resilient

* Optimistic
* Trying to mash up "realist" with "optimist"
* You help me see things from a better perspective
* Optimist

Do you see the patterns? My three character strengths are listening/empathy, resilience/determination, and optimism.

Your People are *brilliant.*

When you identify your strength patterns, type them up, take a screen shot, and keep them as a favorite on your phone. Tape your list to your computer or your bathroom mirror. Memorize them. Take this feedback, and focus on making your strengths even stronger.

These are your gifts. These are your *Super-Powers.*

"The grass is not greener on the other side . . .
It's greener where you water it."
—Robert Fulghum

Happiness Practice

Be aware of three ways we can unconsciously bring ourselves down:

1. Giving that Inner Critic unchecked airtime
2. Holding ourselves to an impossible standard of perfection
3. Comparing ourselves to others who seem to have it all

Shore up your weaknesses, but obsess over your strengths.

6-3-3

- 6—List six people whose opinion you value. If you come up with more than six, go for it. You are a lucky human being.

  1.
  2.
  3.
  4.
  5.
  6.

* **3**—Send them a note, asking, "What are three of my strengths?"

* **3**—Of the list you get back, compile them, and look for three descriptions that are similar. They may not use the exact same words, but look for similarities.

What patterns do you see emerging? Any time you see similar descriptions that reappear at least three times, you know you have a pattern. You may see one pattern. You may see three or four.

* **What can you do to demonstrate your strengths more consistently?**
    -
    -
    -
    -

"I am in competition with no one. I have no desire to play the game of being better than anyone. I am simply trying to be better than the person I was yesterday."

—Jenny Perry

8. Mind Your Words

"Handle them carefully, for words have more power than atom bombs."

—Pearl Strachan Hurd

A while back, my mom asked me to give a talk to her church's women's circle. "Sure," I remember saying. "Let's talk about the topic as we get closer to the date." The next time I went home to visit my family, I asked her about it.

"Mom, do you have any ideas about what you want me to talk about at Susannah Circle?"

"Oh," she said, "I meant to tell you," as she rummaged through a drawer. "Here."

She handed me a professionally printed flyer with big, bold lettering:

"The Most Powerful Words in the World"
Presented by Susan Denny Hall

"The Most Powerful Words in the *World?* The whole *World*? Geez, Mom! That's a lot of pressure. Has this been sent out yet?"

"Oh, come on!" she rolled her eyes. "You're a professional communicator. Companies *pay* you to help them communicate better. You can do this in your sleep."

Okay, so here's the thing. Once I got over those initial questions—

"*How the heck am I going to pull this off?*" and

"*What exactly ARE the most powerful words?*" and

"*What gives me the right to think I even know what they are?*"

—the answer actually came pretty easily.

I've learned some things through my years of helping others tap into their best. And I've had to learn to deal with what many consider one of the most terrifying words they could ever hear. (Yes, the "c" word.) Here's what I've learned:

The most powerful words we speak are the words we speak to ourselves.

You know that soundtrack that's constantly playing in your head? The one that chatters on about everything from "W*hat am I going to make for dinner tonight?*" to *"Do I have time to pick up the laundry before I need to pick the kids at school?"* to that annoying critic—*"You're not good enough, smart enough, young enough, or old enough. You're just not enough."*

Yep, THAT voice. Wouldn't it be wonderful if you could dial the volume WAY down sometimes? Or better yet, hit the mute button?

Well, it turns out that you can.

We can intentionally dial up or dial down the emotional intensity of our words, and the intensity of our emotions will follow.

Words carry emotional weight. They have the power to inspire and move people to great action, to experience great joy and great sorrow.

Have you ever teared up with emotion at something said by a loved one—or even a movie actor?

Have you ever laughed out loud at the memory of something funny a friend said, maybe years ago?

Have you ever found yourself waving your hands emphatically in your car while driving as you think about something someone said that struck a nerve? That person isn't even there with you. But you feel the emotion those words caused all over again just by having the *thought* of it.

Words MOVE us.

In *Psychology Today*, Dr. Andrew Newberg, M.D., in "Words Can Change Your Brain," writes,

"If I were to put you into an MRI scanner (for your brain) and flash the word "NO" for less than one second, you'd see a sudden release of dozens of stress-producing hormones and neurotransmitters. These chemicals immediately interrupt the normal functioning of your brain, impairing logic, reason, language processing, and communication." He goes on, *"Negative thinking is also self-perpetuating, and the more you engage in negative dialogue—at home or at work—the more difficult it becomes to stop."*

In short, words matter. With this research in mind, think of the implications that the words "I can't" have on our brains. How many times do we say this to ourselves until we finally start believing we "can't"? In most cases, when I'm tempted to say, "I can't," what I really mean is "I don't want to." Isn't that a lot more empowering? This way, it's about a choice, not a lack of ability. Ahh, but that means we have to take responsibility for our emotions and actions, doesn't it?

I had a college roommate whose two favorite words were "Amazing" and "Horrible."

"I saw the most *amazing* art show today!"

"My dinner was just *horrible!*"

Here's the danger:

She used those extreme words to describe entire *days.* A tough exam or a bad date, and suddenly the *whole day* was "horrible!" She was a bit of a Drama Queen, and a lot of that is because of the words she used. It's no surprise that her emotions, and her days, had some pretty extreme swings.

Was the entire day horrible? Or was it just a bad moment?

I video-called my dad the other evening and asked him how his day was.

"Oh," he grimaced and shook his head hard. "It was so *ugly* here. Just *miserable!*"

My heart lurched, imagining the grisly aftermath of one of his power-tool projects gone wrong.

"Are you okay?" I jumped, alarmed.

"Me? Sure," he frowned, perplexed at my reaction. "But it rained all day long."

Was your day ugly and miserable? Or just rainy?

Again, it's a decision, isn't it? Simple, but not always easy.

The intensity of our words, both out loud and in our own head *(especially in our own head),* creates the intensity of emotion. When I was diagnosed with the spine tumor, I decided to refer to it as a "blip." First of all, "tumor" was just way too scary a word to even think about, let alone say out loud. And "blip" signified some smallish detour or hurdle that I would surely soon get over. Whether it was true or not, thinking of cancer as a temporary thing that I just needed to get through *helped*. A friend, also diagnosed with a "blip," referred to it as *the* tumor, as opposed to *my* tumor. "I don't want to give it the impression that it's welcome to hang out and stay as long as it wants to," she reasoned.

Cancer is, without a doubt, a "terrifying" and "horrible" disease. But whenever I let myself go there, I felt a painful, visceral reaction.

My heart raced so loudly I could hear it.

I couldn't breathe.

I felt a crushing weight and tension in my chest.

So, I made a decision about the words I was going to use to describe the experience of the "c" word. I decided that cancer (little c) was going to be "inconvenient." Because who wants to face a future that is "terrifying" and "horrible"? I can't handle that.

Now, "inconvenient"? Not ideal, but *that* I can handle.

Try it.

- What if, instead of feeling "*miserable,*" you felt "*a little down*"? How would that change the emotional intensity of the feeling? Would the emotion be dialed up, or down?

- What about instead of being "*worried*" or "*freaked out,*" you felt "*concerned*"?

* Instead of "*furious*," you were "*a little miffed*"?

* Instead of "*overwhelmed*" you "*have a lot going on*"?

* Instead of feeling "*helpless*" or "*paralyzed*," you felt "*challenged.*"

* Instead of "*I can't*," you own up to "*I won't*" or "*I don't want to*"? Or "*I need to learn how to*" *or* "*I need some help.*"

There are times when we want to use emotionally intense words. Sometimes, if I'm having a miserable moment, by gosh, I want everyone to know just how miserable I am! And sometimes we need a good, juicy word for dramatic effect.

It all comes down to a *decision. Do you see the pattern here?*

Ask yourself: Is this word—and the emotion it creates in your body—serving you? If it's not, then change the words you are using in your brain and out loud to dial down the intensity.

On the other hand, there are some emotions that we want to dial up. When that's the case, we can use more highly charged words to dial *up* the intensity.

* What about, instead of feeling "*fine*," you felt "*amazing*"? *Or* "*exceptional*"? How would that elevate your level of happiness?

* What if, instead of "*interested*," you felt "*intrigued*"?

* Instead of "*funny*," you find it "*hilarious*"?

- What if, when someone asks, "*How are you*?" instead of the obligatory "*Fine,*" you answer "*Outstanding*"? Or "*Wonderful*?" How would that make you feel?

Be aware of the words you use and the emotions they create. A simple choice of words can have a profound effect on our sense of self-esteem and have a powerful influence on those around us.

Happiness Practice

This week, pay attention to the words that you and the people around you use. Take special note of the words you say to yourself in your head—the words that you don't even say out loud.

Are these words serving you?

* What is one word you use frequently that may be contributing to stress, pain, unhappiness? If you're not sure, ask your partner or a friend.
    -
    -
    -
    -
* What word could you use instead to dial down the intensity?
    -
    -
    -
    -
* What's one word you use that represents a positive emotion that you want to dial up?
    -
    -
    -
    -

✷ What word can you use to dial up the intensity?

-
-
-
-

✷ Try using these words. How do they feel?

-
-
-
-

Are you writing all of this down? Because you're pretty freakin' brilliant, and you don't want to forget all of these great thoughts in your head.

9. Let It Go

"Pain is inevitable. Suffering is optional."

—Buddha

A few years ago, Tim and I took a cruise to southeast Asia. Elephants, luxury, *and* a trip to Thailand—that's a "three-fer" if there ever was one. If you've ever cruised before, you know that the port talks are part of the enhanced experience. As a learner, I made sure to attend each of the talks to learn about the various ports of call we would be visiting. Later, I would brief Tim over coffee or martinis and enthusiastically share all of the cultural tidbits I had learned.

They say that when the student is ready, the teacher will appear. I could never have known that the teacher I needed most at that time was Marshall Stearn, a short guru in khakis and a polo shirt with a distinct Bronx accent, who gave a series of lectures entitled "Buddhism 101."

He called himself a "Jew Bu."

I thought I was attending a series of lectures to better understand the culture and surroundings that we were exploring. I never expected that I'd end up on a life-changing, introspective journey of overcoming desperate, deep-seated grief. You see, for the past year, I had been working very hard to bury grief over the loss of a beloved friend.

I met Russell in the driveway of a neighbor's home while walking my dog, back in Baltimore. He was moving an exquisite cabinet with intricate woodworking.

"That's stunning," I said. "Did you paint this?"

"I built this," he smiled.

We struck up a conversation over dogs and cabinetry and how everything sounded better with a British accent, which he employed with a deep resonance and easy laugh. We became fast friends. Russell was a Renaissance man. When it came to home interior, he could not only dream it, he could build it. Well, 90% of it. Then his ADD kicked in, and he quickly got bored with the finishing details. Tim and I once bribed him with a birthday party at our house to finish a project. There's nothing like a deadline to push your contractor (and guest of honor) to get the house together. We invited all of his friends and served his favorite red velvet cake with its special birthday message piped elegantly on top in buttercream icing.

JFTFL!*

* Which translated to: *"Just Finish the F-ing Lounge!"*

He never did.

But he came close. To this day, people walk into our home, a comfortable but un-extraordinary suburban colonial, and exclaim "Wow!" when they look up, surprised and delighted by the unanticipated carved ceilings, decorative paint, and custom woodwork.

Russell was a *Good Human Being.*

He was kind and funny and irreverent. And, while Russell Time was its own time zone, when he did show up several hours after the agreed-upon time, he was 100% focused. When Russell spoke with you, you were the only person in the room.

Russell was *present.*

When he died young from a short and intense battle with leukemia, I felt angry and ripped off.

- One day we were laugh-groaning as our dog dipped his tail in black accent paint and wagged his way all around the freshly painted living room.

- The next, Russell was wasting away in a hospital bed, attached to tubes and ventilators, surrounded by many loved ones praying desperately for a miracle.

How could this happen to such a wonderful human being? Wasn't there any sense of fairness in the world? It felt fundamentally *wrong.* Every time I thought of Russell, every time I let myself pause and take in the works of art he had created in our home, I felt angry and ripped off all over again.

Fast forward to a year later. I was sitting in an auditorium on a 4000-passenger cruise ship, listening to a port-of-call lecture. I was taking notes. And bawling my eyes out.

Because Marshall, My Unexpected Teacher, was able to help me see that I was doing a bang-up job of creating a world of suffering for myself. Every time I thought about my friend, which was often, because he basically built the home we live in, I felt—I ***focused***—on the loss and pain. Of course, it was perfectly natural to feel sorrow after the loss of my friend. The problem is that I was *stuck* there, unable to move forward. Without realizing it, through my focus on the pain, I was *choosing* to suffer. And that is the last thing Russell would have wanted. He would have wanted me to think of him with a smile, not anger, with joy, not bitterness.

I would like to tell you that I learned this lesson then, but, apparently, I'm not such a quick study.

I lost my beloved whippet, Chili Pepper, to a tragic hit-and-run accident. I loved his gentle soul as much as any human's. Tim and I had rescued him from a neglect situation and, with patience and time, celebrated every milestone as he learned to trust the human race. Countless times, we greeted our friends at the front door with a handful of treats and strict instructions to "*Look away and let him come to you to take the treat.*" Along with us, they marveled the first time, and every time after, when Pep happily trotted over to greet them with a wag of his tail and a soft nudge of his pointy nose. He grew into a sweet, loving friend, always by my side.

That Friday evening in March, I stayed back to finish curling my hair in anticipation of dinner with Tim at a downtown restaurant, while my husband walked the dogs.

If only I had gone with Tim on that walk that night.

If only he had walked them on a different street.

If only that raccoon hadn't startled them.

If only Pep had had his harness on instead of that collar.

If only the driver of the SUV had seen him.

If only. . . .

I clung hard to that pain and guilt, unable to look at photographs of Pep's sweet, graying face, his adoring, earnest brown eyes. I kept a shrine for him in his favorite sleeping place. His empty dog bed and unused toys in the corner of my closet were a daily reminder of the hole in my heart. Just thinking of him made my heart hurt and my eyes fill up with anguish.

Not for two weeks.

Not for two months.

For two *years.*

This time, my Teacher was a highly empathetic animal lover, introduced to me by CJ, Tim's sister and my dear friend. She helped me see that I was hanging on to the grief and guilt because I so desperately wanted to hang on to *him*. The pain was all I had left of him. If I lost that, then what would I have?

But we don't have to hold onto pain to hold onto someone we love.

I realized, once again, I was unconsciously *choosing* to suffer. So finally, I decided to choose a different reaction. And, I'm not exaggerating about this: the moment I *decided,* the suffering diminished. Just like that.

Now, when I think of Pep, it's bittersweet. I still miss him. But I no longer torment myself by replaying that nightmarish Friday evening scene in my head over and over and over again. I replay how he *lived.* If my thoughts go dark, I immediately and intentionally refocus my memory on one of the many moments of joy we had together over so many years.

Why do we hang on to pain, reliving it over and over again?

We cling to pain and hurts that happened years, even decades, ago. I remember having a conversation with a woman lamenting about her ex-husband. Her face screwed up in anger and her shoulders drew up around her ears—the pain still very real and present in her mind and body.

"I'm so sorry. When did this all happen?" I asked.

"Twenty-three years ago," she spat. "I'll never forgive him."

Twenty-three years. That's a long time to let suffering poison your days and steal your joy.

In no way am I minimizing the pain and suffering of loss. I'm not a grief counselor or a psychiatrist, but I know firsthand how critical it is to mourn and grieve and **feel it all** for as long as you need to feel it.

The question is: Are you stuck there?

Pain is inevitable. Suffering is optional.

And so, the biggest loss of my life—my mother.

The human being who had loved me the most and the longest, from before I was born. My mom was a seeker, a poet, an artist, a force. She was my cheerleader, travel buddy, and therapist. She was my hero, my irreplaceable friend. My mom worked wit and whimsy and wisdom with her words. I am feeling the ache of her absence as I write these pages. I have always known I couldn't imagine a world without her in it, and so I won't. I keep her very close to my heart.

And whenever something reminds me of her—*a friendly stranger striking up a conversation in the grocery-store checkout line, spring robins on the lawn, bold jewelry, songs and starlit nights, a mother and daughter walking arm in arm, (any) holiday napkins or decor, books stacked up like possibilities on a nightstand, summertime fireflies, field bouquets of Queen Anne's lace and Black-eyed Susans, a laughter-filled room, a splash of art, spontaneous singing or whistling*—I stop and feel her presence in my heart. Oh, I have some epic Mom-cries, and they always seem to grab me when I'm not expecting it. My eyes welled up at Starbuck's just the other day. I can't have a latte without seeing her at the front door as I roll my suitcase in for a weekend visit, greeting me with a delighted hug and an "Oh! I'm so happy to see you, honey! Where's my latte?"

The pain is undeniably real. I miss her with an ache that is sometimes so sudden and so fierce that it takes my breath away. But I *choose* not to let the suffering itself take over and drive. I *choose t*o steer my thoughts and memories and think of her with that sparkle of joy that was so much a part of her. I choose to feel it all. Fully.

But I cling to the love, not the pain.

Happiness Practice

"Feel the pain, and let it go."

—Mary Mundt

* Is there a loss, a hurt, or pain that you have been clinging to?
  -
  -
  -
  -
  -

* How long ago did this occur?
  -
  -
  -
  -
  -

* How is this serving you?
  -
  -
  -
  -
  -

✷ What is clinging to this pain costing you?

-
-
-
-

✷ How can you focus your thoughts, your memories to serve you better? To create happier moments and take a more positive meaning from this?

-
-
-
-

✷ What is one of your favorite memories that you can focus on to bring less suffering? Perhaps even joy?

-
-
-
-

Child of the Universe

I am a child of the universe.
My feet don't need to walk on cement.
They can dance on the Milky Way.
My heels can kick up stardust.
No need to sigh or lament.

I can open my arms
And scoop up atoms, spinning planets.
Breathe the breath of unknown forefathers,
Dip my fingers in sunspots.

I will stay for a while.
When I decide to leave
I will sparkle with
The energy that surrounds me,
And is given generously and freely
From an unending source.

"Whimsy," by Marian Denny

10. The Power of Progress

"The journey of a thousand miles begins with one step."

—Lao Tzu

When my mom died suddenly, my father, along with the rest of us, was devastated. He had lost not only his love and partner in life, he had lost his morning-paper-puzzle partner, his social director, the comedian to his straight man, the soundtrack that accompanied life with constant song, the sparkle in his day, his best friend.

From a practical standpoint, he had also lost his caregiver. My dad is disabled and unable to walk even a step or two due to neurological issues, probably from jumping out of too many airplanes while in the Army or breaking too many bones from falling out of too many trees and off of too many bicycles and ladders for too many years. In addition to reeling from deep loss and struggling to navigate the idea of living in a world without Marian, we had to come up with a Plan B for Dad.

But it was too painful to plan. We were struggling just to breathe.

We did, however, manage to take just one baby step.

"Dad," I asked, "What if you came down to Florida for a few weeks? You and Mom loved it there. One of us can fly down with you. I have friends who aren't using their condo and would let you use it. It's handicap accessible. And you can get out of the winter for a while."

While he thought about it, my brain continued to spin.

* *Could we still get him into assisted living? And if so, which one?*

* *And could he afford it?*

* *We'll have to sell the house. Sixty years of stuff. Ugh! How will we tackle that?!*

* *What about in-home care?*

* *Mom did everything for him. She did all the cooking, the finances. . . . He doesn't even make himself a bowl of cereal.*

* *Where is the checkbook? And the financial statements?*

* *When are his doctor's appointments?*

* *How is he going to even function?!*

I was stacking up a mountain of stress on top of a precipice of profound grief. This time, my brother Steve was the voice of reason.

"It will all come together eventually," he said. "Let's just get him to Florida, out of the cold, and into the sunshine. We can worry about what happens next another day."

One step at a time. *Brilliant.*

In the future in our minds, Dad, who was 84 years old at the time, would be living in a nice Assisted Living Center in Allentown, Pennsylvania, where family and lifelong friends could visit him. He'd have caregivers who would take him to Physical Therapy, clean his apartment, and make hot meals for him every day. They might even get him to eat an occasional vegetable now and then. He's a quiet man and would enjoy playing bridge, reading, and, on Friday evenings, going to the Activity Room for cookies and punch.

Here's how it really happened:

Three weeks into his stay, Dad bought the little one-bedroom condo for sale in Florida next to my friends' place. He tricked the place out with grab bars and ramps, and hired a person to come in every two weeks to clean and grocery shop. He has a credit card and an Amazon account, and is not shy about using either, as evidenced by the rowing machine, new pullout sofa, and circular saw in the middle of his living room. He bought a crockpot and a mini oven, and taught himself to cook. First, he dabbled with bacon and eggs, and then beef barbecue, before moving on to more advanced meat-based cuisine: pork roast and sauerkraut. He's a sociable man and enjoys playing bridge at the clubhouse, watching vintage B-rated horror films and, on Friday evenings, scootering down to the Tiki Hut at the pool for hotdogs and $3 Manhattans. We talk every day and, as far as I know, his daily diet does not include one vegetable, other than potato chips, which he still insists qualify.

The point is that none of us, certainly not my father, could have imagined this future for him. It seemed impossibly unattainable when we were in such a deep state of shell shock. Granted, it took a small village and lots of organizing to get him set up—but it all happened. *One step at a time.*

You don't have to have it all figured out to move forward—just take the first step.

When going through a challenging time, facing a big hurdle, or contemplating doing something new, there are two different ways to focus:

Option 1: To Freak Yourself Out:
Focus on the *obstacles* in your way.

Option 2: To Make Progress and Maintain Sanity
Focus on the *next step* toward your goal.

Having personally researched and experimented extensively with Option #1, I wholeheartedly endorse Option #2.

There's a process we all use, consciously or unconsciously, for making progress and gaining momentum:

Power Momentum Process

Step 1: Decide—Resolve to think and do something (even one, small thing) a little differently

Step 2: Act—Take frequent, small, consistent actions every day, until you make progress toward your goal

Step 3: Forgive yourself—When you fall off the wagon, get right back on track

When I was recovering from spine surgery, I couldn't bend, lift, twist, sit, or walk up or down stairs for several months. The list of my "don'ts" was a hundred times as long as my "do's."

Every day I tried to do just a tiny something more than I had the day before. Compared to my normal activity, my goals felt ridiculously minuscule. Some days, I took three steps back, but I did my best to focus on where I was *going*. I didn't compare myself to where I had *been* prior to the surgery. Though molehills suddenly felt like mountains, I celebrated each small accomplishment for the milestone I knew it was.

- The first time I got back on my spin bike, I rode for four minutes. You would have thought I'd won the Tour de France.
- The first time I walked to the corner of my block and back, Tim jumped up and down and cheered. Our neighbor yelled to us from across the street, "Did you guys win the lottery or something?"

"Yes!" Tim shouted back.

Making Progress Makes Us Happy

Think back to a recent day when you fell into bed contented, feeling accomplished and happy. I bet you made progress that day. Maybe it was making a dent in that project at work, cooking a special dinner for your family, practicing a musical instrument or a second language, painting a wall, or planting flowers in the pots on your front step. Whatever it was, we human beings like moving forward. Even if it's a step or two here and a step or two there, we are happier when we are making progress.

Regardless of your age, it's never too early, or too late, to start. As long as we are alive, we can make progress.

- My dad, at 84, moved a thousand miles away and started a brand-new chapter in his life.

- A family friend, at 73, got her first kitten and fell so in love with her that she started a non-profit rescue.

- Another friend left his high-stress, high-profile career in Manhattan's finance district, got his real estate license at 50, and started a whole new career selling luxury real estate in a beautiful southern resort town.

Maybe you're 23 or 33, not 73. It doesn't matter how old or young we are. It's never too early or too late to make progress.

Joe, my brother-in-law, had always wanted to play the guitar. With a young family and a full-time job, he didn't have a lot of extra time. But he committed to practicing for thirty minutes a day, five days a week. Eventually he got so good that he started performing at open-mike nights to rousing applause. And not just from his family—from strangers, too. That small, consistent, daily commitment added up to big progress over time.

Do you know what finally made me decide that I could write this book? When I took the first step and gave myself *permission* to write just one page a day. Writing a *Whole Entire Book* seemed overwhelming. But a page a day? Now, *that*, I can do. And, as I'm sure you've experienced, a small commitment to progress—whether it's a page a day, a fifteen-minute walk, twenty minutes to unclutter the garage, thirty minutes to tackle that business project—can often very willingly turn into more time once we Decide, Act, and begin to pick up some momentum.

I'll leave you with one more story about the Power of Progress. I am writing this chapter during a tumultuous time in our world. Divisiveness and racial tension are not just in the headlines, they are at the doorstep of every home and community in our nation. Like so many, I felt heartsick at the polarization and hostility that is boiling and bubbling up everywhere. And, like so many, I felt helpless. After all, racism is a layered and complex problem, born of multiple insidious causes and deeply embedded in our culture over centuries of time.

I'm just one person. ***What can I possibly do?***

And then I heard about a woman who was terrified of the police in her community. She could have kept on being terrified and avoiding the police, and no one would have thought less of her. Instead, do you know what she did?

She invited the police into her home for tea.

Here is one person, willing to take one small action to tackle a Big Problem in a manner that is simple, personal, and pure-hearted. Who knows what kind of ripple effect her actions will have out in the world? I have to believe this is progress.

I decided to ask myself a better question: ***What can I do that's possible?***

So I invited the ladies in my neighborhood to a Tuesday-evening virtual get-together. The purpose was not to try to tackle world issues. The purpose was to connect with others in our little community, and, in doing so, maybe—just maybe—create some bonds instead of barriers. I sent the email invitation to more than sixty households. We had fourteen women on the call, with the unanimous decision to schedule another. Since then, I have received emails and calls from at least eleven additional neighbors who were unable to join or had heard about it afterwards and want to join the next call. Many of these neighbors—whose names I hadn't even known before—have lived in my neighborhood for more than twenty years! At the very least, our walks around the community are far more pleasant now. They are longer, too, with spontaneous stops to chat with Angie, and Candace, and Carolyn—fabulous friends I didn't know I had, and who have lived right next to me this whole time.

Here's to progress.

Happiness Practice

If you're stuck, ask yourself, "Am I focusing on the obstacles? Is there just one, first step I can take?"

Think of the Power Momentum Process:

1. **Decide**—What's something in your life that you want to improve or change? Or perhaps something that you want in your life that currently isn't there?
   -
   -
   -
   -

2. **Act**—What's one small step you can take to make progress in this area?
   -
   -
   -
   -

   * If it involves a time commitment, what's a reasonable and conservative amount of time you could dedicate to this?
     -
     -
     -
     -

3. Forgive yourself and get back on track

- Who do you need to reach out to help support you with this step?
  -
  -
  -
  -

- When will you do this?
  -
  -
  -
  -

- Why is it important to you?
  -
  -
  -
  -

Dear Neighbor,

I have lived in our neighborhood for more than twenty years. My husband and I fell in love with our home, but also with the diversity and friendliness of our community, tucked away quietly like a tree-lined gem, yet so close to everything. Through that time, some things have changed, and some things have stayed the same. You may have seen me walking one of our greyhound dogs. We may have stopped to chat with each other, smiled a hello, or waved in passing.

This past year, I have been alternately moved, shocked, and brought to my knees by the power that individuals can have on our lives and in our communities. I believe community and peace start at home. I believe all of us, regardless of gender, color, or political inclination, have more in common to bring us together than disparities that push us apart.

And I believe in the power of women. I was lucky enough to be raised by a strong woman, and I have friends who are strong women, making a positive difference in the world.

So, let's do something. Let's take a small action to reach out to each other, as women, as neighbors, and maybe as friends.

Below is an invitation to a virtual Happy Hour. Please stop in for a few minutes, for an hour, to meet and re-meet some new friends. No pressure, no politics. Grab a cup of tea or glass of wine, and let's get to know each other a little better.

I'm looking forward to seeing you!

Susan Hall

PS: Please share this invitation with your fabulous neighbors. Not everyone had their email on the community portal. Every woman in our neighborhood is welcome. Spread the word!

11. Feel It All

"Never apologize for showing your feelings.
When you do, you are apologizing for the truth."
—Jose N. Harris

Santa came through our neighborhood on his firetruck, a highly anticipated annual event sponsored by our local fire department. Santa had an app this year, and Tim tracked him on his phone as the little red dot made its way through the cul de sacs and squares that represented our surrounding neighborhoods. We heard the sirens in the distance drawing closer, fading into the night again, and then rounding the corner, until we could finally see the flashing lights.

"He's coming!" Tim announced like a delighted five-year old, grabbing his coat and dashing out of the front door. I grabbed mine, too, and followed him out onto the icy front step. And promptly burst into tears.

Well. What was ***that*** *all about?!*

I stood there in the cold, trying to silence the sobs, hoping no one would notice as Tim ran out with our neighbors to greet Santa and his team.

What was going on here? I love Santa on a firetruck! I love the way our neighbors impulsively gather on this special night, hurrying out of their warm-lit homes, quickly pulling on coats and scarves, greeting each other with excited grins, children of all ages and religions waving and shouting and feeling the spirit of the winter moment. But in that instant, it was as if every holiday childhood-charged emotion swelled up and came crashing down on me.

- I was four years old, riding high on my dad's shoulders to get a glimpse of Pip the Christmas Mouse at his annual appearance in the snowy window at Hess's department store on Hamilton Street.

- I was five, eyes wide, kneeling on my bed with my hands and face pressed against the cold glass of my bedroom window, painstakingly searching the skies for any sign of a sleigh, an antler, a red glow.

- Now I was sleeping with my blanket in front of Mom and Dad's bedroom door, knowing "It's too early to go downstairs. Wait until 7 am!" but determined to be there and ready when the call went up.

- Finally, after the longest night of my short little life, I could hear Mom and Dad stirring. And I gathered with my brothers, humming with excitement and impatience in our jammies and robes and slippers at the top of the stairs.

Few traditions pack as much emotional punch as cherished holiday rituals, whatever they may be. For me, it was my father's Christmas Eve reading of "'Twas the Night before Christmas," the dining-room table, covered with white sheets and twelve kinds of Christmas cookies cooling from the oven, the proud and reverent sounds of traditional Christmas carols being sung in a church filled with candlelight and awe. All are treasured. Because, for me, Christmas will always be about family, and warmth, and wonder.

But that's all changed now.

Mom, who kept Christmas in her heart for all of us, is gone.

Dad is 1000 miles away.

The family home has been emptied and sold.

We are adrift, struggling to find an anchor in new traditions and rituals.

And I am feeling bereft.

We can't be happy all the time.

We human beings are not one-dimensional creatures. We are far more complex, with a full range of emotions and feelings. Twenty-seven plus, as a matter of fact, according to a study by the University of California at Berkeley. These include the usual suspects, as well as entrancement, confusion, awe, excitement, joy, and nostalgia, all of which were jumbled into a supercharged emotional cocktail that was too much for me to contain that night on that icy front step.

Sometimes, the best way to truly deal with pain is to go straight through it. Our culture admonishes us to "shake it off," or "get over it." We feel something we don't like and distract ourselves with our phones and devices, rather than confronting it head on. Yet, when we ignore or push down our feelings, they tend to "boomerang" and leak out of the cracks. Or flood, in my case.

Experiencing our feelings is part of what it means to have a full life. You deserve to be kind to yourself and give yourself time, just as you would empathize and be kind with a loved one going through a difficult time. Allowing ourselves to feel fully helps us to heal and move forward. To do this, we need to slow down, reflect, and allow ourselves to sit with our feelings for a while.

That night, I took out my journal and wrote. I dug deep to peel back the layers and get to the true cause of my emotional outburst. (See **Observe Your Thoughts**.) There is something validating and calming in the act of naming or labeling our emotions. Emotions come and go like waves. Sometimes we have to ride the wave instead of trying to fight it and risk getting pulled into the undertow.

Here's what I discovered:

That powerful surge of emotion I thought was bereavement? When I unpacked it, it was that, but also something much more complicated and wonderful. At the heart of all that emotion was an immense tidal wave of love and gratitude.

I am so grateful I had all of those Christmases.

I am so grateful for those warm family memories.

I'm grateful knowing that we will somehow make new traditions and hold our loved ones in our hearts and memories, even if we can't be together.

So, I will sing along to my mother's favorite, "Silent Night," and continue to hold the joy and magic of the season close.

And I will laugh, and cry, as Santa makes his way down the street on his Christmas firetruck.

Feeling It All isn't just for difficult emotions. Never miss an opportunity to celebrate.

When Tim and I flew to Asia a few years ago, we braced ourselves for a crowded, uncomfortable flight, knowing we would be sitting upright, dazed and sleepless for more than sixteen hours. This was on top of the twelve hours of cabs, trains, and automobiles that it had taken for us to get to the airport. As we waited in the International terminal, we heard our names being called over the intercom system. Tim and I looked at each other with the same thought: *"This is either really good, or really, really bad."*

"Mr. and Mrs. Hall? Yes, we've had a few cancellations and we would like to move you from coach to business class. Are you amenable to this?"

I'm sure we looked stupefied as we mentally double and triple verified the definition of "amenable."

"Uh, yes," I stammered, pinching my leg. "We would be very amenable to this."

For those of you who have flown internationally in business class, you are no doubt smiling in a knowing way right now. Because business class on an international flight means not only real china and cutlery, but better food and champagne (!). It also means eye masks, slippers, and, most important, our very own sleeping pods.

In which each of us could fully recline.

In a bed.

And *sleep*.

Tim and I very calmly took our re-issued tickets, walked around the corner . . . and jumped up and down like pre-schoolers over cookies and bug juice. We danced a gleeful, little arm-in-arm do-si-do. In both directions. We did The Wave. Then The Sprinkler. We pulled out all of our silliest dance moves right there in Terminal 4 at John F. Kennedy International Airport, with many Very Serious People passing by. We were having such a good time with our celebratory antics that, when we caught the eye of a grinning onlooker, we celebrated even harder. Okay, not the most proper adult behavior. But it sure was fun.

There are the big celebrations, of course. But what about the little, everyday moments? How can we make them more magical?

* A surprise call from an old friend.

* Free cookie samples at the grocery store.

* Progress on a school report card.

- A bright, sunshiny day.
- Your luggage appears intact on the airport baggage carousel.
- You beat the Friday night traffic home.

Remember, even our worst days have just twenty-four hours.

Allow Yourself to Feel It All. Take a moment to appreciate, to celebrate those special moments, and maybe even to jump.

Happiness Practice

* The next time you're feeling a difficult emotion, allow yourself to sit quietly with it for ten to fifteen minutes, without talking. It often helps to write down what you are feeling.

  1. Is there someone you can talk with who can listen or help?
     -
     -
  2. When you're ready to carry on, leaf through this book. Which one or two Happiness Practices appeal to you? Try it out. My go-to's? **Gratitude** and **Be Kindhearted.**
     -
     -

* What can you celebrate today?
  -
  -

* Who can you involve?
  -
  -

* How might you do this? *I recommend cake.*
  -
  -

12. Observe Your Thoughts

"Don't believe everything you think."

—Allan Lokos

Today, I woke up crabby.

After I snapped at Tim, grumbled through a project I had procrastinated, responded a little too sharply to the customer-service person who didn't give me the answer I wanted to hear, and ignored my dog, who just wanted to play, I got sick of my grumpy self. The day was halfway over. I was never going to get this day back again. I *know* better. Time to look all this grumpiness in the face and get my Happy back.

Taking our own emotional temperature can help us deal with the thing that's really bugging us or stealing our joy.

Here's a way to do this pretty easily. I call it "Digging for Truth." I thought of calling it "Digging for Crap," which it kind of is, but Tim said that didn't sound very elegant.

Either way, the process involves asking yourself, "What else?" several times, until you hit bedrock truth. Once you uncover the real reason for your mood, you can *do* something about it. Even if you can't change the situation, you can always decide to change how you feel about it.

Here's an example of how this worked for me:

Okay, self, why am I so irritable today? What's the real reason behind all this crabbiness? What am I ***not*** *happy about?*

"Well," my grumpy brain answered immediately, *"I didn't sleep well last night."* True. Okay, what else?

"The bathroom scale was NOT happy." Also true. What else?

"I am overwhelmed with this stupid project." Okay, what else?

"Tim has made dinner four nights in a row, and I should be the one to go to the store this time and make dinner, and I don't have time because of this stupid project!"

Hmmm. Interesting. Okay, go on. . . . what else?

This time the answers didn't come so fast. I thought for a full four seconds.

"I'm worried about my dad. He's living alone and had another fall, involving 911."

And?

"And I feel guilty because I'm not there to help. I'm his only daughter. I should be able to fix this."

As soon as this thought registered in my brain, my eyes welled up.

Bingo! We have a winner.

Now, there are a few things going on here. But it all boils down to:

1. Feeling like I had no control, and

2. Worry and guilt over my dad

If you've read **Progress**, you already know some things about my father:

* He is very clear and confident in making his own choices. Despite being wheelchair bound, at 84 years of age, my dad *chose* to pick up his life and move to Florida after my mom died.

* He *chose* to move 1000 miles away from family so he could enjoy the sunshine and a new chapter in his life.

* He *chose* to buy a little condo and live independently.

* His mind is sharp, and he is capable of making (mostly) good decisions for himself, despite his propensity to buy power tools and use them in creative ways for which they were probably not intended or designed. Also, a choice.

So, on this grumpy day, I was doing a "trifecta" of un-happiness creating:

1. **Stacking multiple negatives**—the number on the scale, procrastinated project, a bad night's sleep, etc.

2. **Using emotionally intense negative words in my head and out loud,** like "overwhelmed" and "stupid."

3. **Blaming events for causing my bad mood.** For example, "I feel guilty because the *project* is making me not

cook dinner for my husband." "I'm grumpy because I didn't sleep last night."

See how we do this?

You may be familiar with Daniel Goleman's brilliant work on Emotional Intelligence, which is "*the capacity to be aware of, control, and express one's emotions, and to handle interpersonal relationships judiciously and empathetically.*" An emotionally intelligent individual is highly conscious of his or her own emotions, even negativity, and able to identify and *manage* them.

1. The first step is to figure out what is at the heart of our anger, frustration, or crabbiness.

2. Then, we can choose whether or not to take some action on the things we *can* actually control and do our best to let go of the things we have no control over.

On this particular grumpy day, I had my pity party then *decided* it was time for this party to be over. So, I took my dog for a long walk outside, called my dad to make sure he hadn't killed himself with his new power drill (which he hadn't), and ordered takeout for Tim and me for dinner. This also included dessert, which didn't help with my bathroom-scale issue but, come on, sometimes cheesecake just helps.

Happiness Practice

Digging for Truth/Crap

1. The next time you are feeling a negative emotion—angry, crabby, frustrated—STOP.
2. Ask yourself, "WHY am I feeling this way?" Write it down.
   -
   -
   -
   -
3. Once your brain comes up with an answer (which it will because you are incredibly smart), ask "What else?" Ask again.
   -
   -
   -
   -
4. Keep asking that "What else?" question until it hits the mark. You'll know when it does because it will touch a nerve and ring true.
   -
   -
   -

5. Then, ask yourself, "Is this something within my control? Can I do anything to make this feel better? If not, can I live this with this?"
    -
    -
    -
    -

6. What is one small thing you can do NOW to feel happier about this? Write it down. Extra points for actually DO-ing it!
    -
    -
    -
    -

Check out the **Decide Happy Quick Reference Guide** to see which practices apply. Fan Faves: **Progress, Gratitude, Control, Stack Life In Your Favor, Be Gentle with Yourself**

13. Be Kindhearted

"Be kind whenever possible.
It is always possible."
—Dalai Lama

When was the last time you felt bad about doing something nice for someone?

I'm guessing the answer is in the vicinity of: **Never.**

It feels good to help someone out or do something kind, doesn't it?

According to the Mayo Clinic Health System, *"Physiologically, kindness can positively change your brain. Being kind boosts serotonin, oxytocin, and dopamine, which are neurotransmitters in the brain that give you feelings of satisfaction and well-being, and cause the pleasure/reward centers in your brain to light up."*

An act of kindness lights up the recipient as well. Giving makes us happy.

Sometimes one small act of caring can change a person's life.

Several years ago, I received a letter in the mail with a very official-looking seal from a university, postmarked Marietta,

Georgia. I didn't know anyone at this university, or in Marietta, Georgia, for that matter.

I was intrigued.

When I opened the envelope, inside was a graduation announcement from the university and a note in an unfamiliar hand. I quickly scanned the signature for the name, also unfamiliar, and checked the envelope again to make sure the address was mine. It was.

The note was from a young man named Brian who had just graduated from (surprise) this university. He was writing to thank me for helping him change his life. "Thanks to your kindness and wisdom," he wrote, "I was able to find the courage to follow my dream to become a chiropractor despite challenging, personal obstacles."

Wow, talk about a hit of oxytocin.

Here's the thing:

Until the moment I read his note, I did not remember Brian.

I did not remember our conversation.

In fact, I had pretty much forgotten all about the conference I had attended where Brian and I met and apparently had this life-altering conversation.

Yet somehow, that chance encounter had helped to change the course of his life.

I stretched my memory, recalling that he had come from a long line of prominent heart surgeons. His father and grandfather expected him, the only son of an only son, to follow in their esteemed footsteps. His parents must have viewed him as radical, with his passion for alternative medicine. Thinking back to that interaction with Brian, it wasn't even what most people would call a "conversation."

I had listened. I had listened and asked a few questions to understand, not to fix anything. That's it. But in the space between the words, he re-discovered and articulated his own strength and made a *decision*. And that decision inspired him to take the action necessary to change the path of his life.

"We rise by lifting others," Robert Ingersoll, the great 19th-century orator, wrote.

Who has lifted you up? Who has been there for you in a difficult moment to show that they care?

I can think of so many teachers, mentors, associates, and friends who have lifted me up. They said or did something that they might not have been aware of at exactly the right time—when I needed it most. We never know what kind of ripples our actions will have in the world.

My mom used to tell me, when I was being crabby, *"Stop whining about yourself and go do something for someone else!"*

I'm sure she was tired of my complaining when she said it, but her words had ripples. That is some of the best advice I've ever received.

It's really hard to be down on yourself when you're doing something up for someone else. Try it. Whether it's the shots of oxytocin and dopamine your brain is giving you, or it's the happy distraction, when we are truly focused on The Other, it's virtually impossible to be preoccupied with ourselves.

Giving just feels good.

And, as we've all given, and we've all benefited from others' generosity, we know that there are many ways to care. Whether by volunteering our time and energy, or giving money to a cause we believe in, or doing something kind for someone in the moment, we affect people's lives in ways we may never know.

"No one is useless in the world who lightens the burden of another."

—Charles Dickens

My colleague and friend Lisa-Marie recently completed a "Dri-Tri," which is basically a triathlon in the gym. While it doesn't include the swimming event of a triathlon, it's still an incredibly strenuous test of strength, fitness, and endurance. The fifteen or so competitors sweated it out and cheered each other on as they finished their heats and saw their names pop up triumphantly on the leader board.

Except for Amy. Amy was struggling.

She had stuck the landing on the 300 pushups and burpees and emptied out all of her reserves in the rowing heat. Now, she was slogging along on the treadmill, so far behind that her co-athletes had given up cheering for her. They were all standing around feeling bad for her, feeling impatient, feeling guilty for feeling impatient, and quietly waiting for her to either finish or give up. Ouch.

"It was really awkward," groaned Lisa-Marie. "I felt so bad for her. I finished last the first time I did the event, and it was so painful."

So, do you know what she did?

After expending every ounce of energy *she* had on the event, Lisa-Marie hopped back on the treadmill next to Amy. "Come on, Amy!" she laughed purposefully. "We are going to finish this race *together.*"

As soon as he saw Lisa-Marie get back on the treadmill, another competitor jumped back on as well. Then another. Then another. Within minutes, *every single one* of those competitors surrounded and supported Amy on their respective treadmills, some walking forward, some backward, some jogging, some dancing.

"It felt like a party," said Lisa-Marie. "A really exhausting, sweaty party. But a party!"

And that is how Amy finished her first Dri-Tri.

You know how, when someone does something unexpectedly kind for you, you immediately want to be kind right back?

I love Simon Sinek's definition of faith: *"It's knowing that we're all on the same team. We just don't know who the other players are."*

We are all on the same team.

This ripple effect of giving and kindness-doing is a powerful force, one that is innate in all of us as humans. We need only to pause and remember to shift the spotlight from ourselves to another.

"Never believe that a few caring people
can't change the world.
For, indeed, that's all who ever have."
—Margaret Mead

Tim did a special magic show recently for a man named Clyde. Clyde and his extensive family were gathered from around the country to celebrate his 103rd birthday. While he presided over the festivities from his wheelchair, Clyde didn't let age rob him of the twinkle in his eye (or a second helping of cake).

"There was something about him. He was just so full of life," Tim shared with me later. "I'm sure he's been asked a thousand times, but I had to ask him, 'What's your secret? Not just to a long life, but to a long, *happy* life.'"

Clyde didn't hesitate.

"Every day we have a new chance to make a difference in the world, no matter how big or how small. We are either helping, or we're hurting. By doing nothing to help, we're not using our gifts, and that's hurting. Every night before I go to sleep, I ask myself, "Clyde, did you leave the world a little bit better today than how you found it?"

Did you leave the world a little bit better today than how you found it?

That's a great litmus test, isn't it? The happiest people I know are also some of the busiest, and yet they find time to care, to give, to pay it forward. We can't control the world, but we *can* control how we move and respond within our own sphere of influence, no matter how small or large our contributions may seem at the time.

My friend Bob volunteers his time and energy at an animal rescue called "Starfish." They transport animals from high-kill shelters into their hub in the Chicago area, where they are bathed and vetted, and then transported to other shelters or foster homes until they find a permanent home.

"Why do they call the rescue group 'Starfish'?" I asked. "Because they have arms like a starfish that reach out to so many other shelters?"

"Well, that's true," he agreed. "But the real inspiration for the name was that old story of the boy with the starfish on the beach."

I must have looked puzzled, because he elaborated.

"One day a man was walking along the beach and came across a young boy. It had just stormed, and there were hundreds of starfish washed up on the shore. He watched for several minutes as the little boy painstakingly picked up starfish, one at a time, and threw them back into the ocean. Finally, the man said, "You know, there are hundreds of starfish here. More than you can ever save. You can't make a difference." The little boy bent down and picked up another starfish, tossing him gently into the tide. He replied, "I can for this one."

We affect others' lives in ways we may never know.

Everyone you encounter may be fighting a battle you know nothing about.

I was fortunate to land with parents who valued thoughtfulness and giving back to their community and friends. While I've tried to carry those values forward in life, my experience with cancer ratcheted up my focus. It's just really important to be kind. Some people wear their struggles and battle scars visibly. But for most of us, it's an inside job.

If I get impatient with someone and feel sharp words on the tip of my tongue, Tim will catch the glint in my eye and say, "Alicia." That's shorthand for *"Be gentle. You have no idea what's happening in this person's life right now."*

We met Alicia just one time, but it was memorable.

It was January 1 of a brand-new year and, after having slept in, Tim and I went out for brunch to a new restaurant, thoughts of pancakes and mimosas dancing in our heads. Apparently, we were not the only ones who wanted to extend the holidays. The restaurant was packed and frenetic, with an hour-plus wait. Just as we were turning to leave, two people got up from their stools at the bar, where they were also serving food. We fist bumped each other at our luck and grabbed the seats, pushing away the stacks of dirty plates until the server could clear them. Having both been servers/bartenders in another life, we were patient. To a point.

Fifteen minutes went by.

Then another five.

I caught the server's eye for the third time, and she nodded from the other end of the bar, clearly exasperated. Another ten minutes went by, and, just when we were ready to leave and resign ourselves to whatever was in our pantry, Alicia came over to acknowledge us.

There was no "I'm sorry for the delay." No "Thanks for waiting."

Alicia's first words were a clipped "Yeah. Waddya want?"

Now, if you've read **Stacking,** you know I get "hangry." *Although that's really no excuse for poor behavior now, is it?* I felt indignation narrow my eyes and sharp words flood my mouth. Alicia put her hands to her face and, in an unexpected shift, burst into tears, instantly vaporizing my impatience.

"I'm so sorry," she said, her shoulders shaking with emotion. "I haven't slept in three days. My daughter was just diagnosed with MS, and she fell down the stairs again, and my husband is deployed, and she's with the neighbor so I can work an extra shift, and . . . and . . . it's just too much."

I took a deep breath. Like so many of us, I know all about Too Much.

"It's okay," I immediately assured her. "This is literally a champagne problem, for us to wait a few minutes for mimosas and brunch . . . "

As the restaurant settled down, we proceeded to get to know the human being that is Alicia. We even stacked the plates while she checked out the diners sitting next to us.

After listening to Alicia's story, I regretted that sting in my eye. I was grateful that, by good fortune and timing, the bite of my words never had a chance to escape. We never know the battles those around us are fighting.

What if we just assumed and acted as if everyone is struggling with something?

What if we assumed positive intent?

Instantly, others' actions would take on a different **Meaning**, wouldn't they?

And we might respond more graciously, more kindly, more gently. Our softer hearts and subsequent actions would soften the hearts of others. And they, in turn, might act more charitably toward others.

Our world has become even louder, more frenetic, more tumultuous. It's easy to slide into a feeling of helplessness.

"I'm one person. what can I possibly do?"

What if, instead, we flipped the question:
"I'm one person. What can I do that's *possible*?"

There are so many ways we can acknowledge and respect our neighbors and those around us:

1. Listen and be present

2. Hold the door for the person behind or in front of you

3. Say "Please" and "Thank you." A lot

4. Wave the car on in front of you

5. Take a meal to someone who is going through a tough time. And spend time with them

6. Pull your neighbor's trashcan out of the steet on trash pick-up day

7. Send a heartfelt note. Leave a text, voicemail or voice-text just to let someone know you are thinking of them

8. Be over-the-top generous with your time, insight and expertise

9. Leave a friend's favorite flowers, or fresh oranges, or anything that reminds you of them in a special way, on their doorstep

10. Teach someone. Mentor another
11. Keep pace with the person you're with so you walk, jog, skate, skip—together
12. Leave a note on your loved one's car windshield or under their pillow before taking that business trip
13. Look into your loved one's eyes when you talk
14. Offer to drive an older person to the doctor or grocery store. Or pick up groceries for them while you are there anyway
15. Give. Serve. Contribute. Help

The list is endless.

Love is a *verb*. Kindness doesn't have to take a lot of time or cost anything. But it does takes *intention* and *attention* and *action*. And with a little more of each, we will leave the day, and the world, a little bit better than how we found it.

"And in the end, the love you take is equal to the love you make."

—The Beatles

Happiness Practice

✷ What is a cause that is important to you? Why?

-
-
-
-
-

What action can you take to help with this cause? No good deed is too small.

-
-
-
-
-

When will you do this?

-
-
-
-

Is there someone you know who is hurting? What's one small act of kindness you can take to show them you care? When will you do this?

-
-
-
-

Is there someone in your life you care about but haven't communicated with in a while?

•

•

•

•

How can you reconnect with them?

•

•

•

•

When?

•

•

•

•

The next time your reaction to an interaction is anger or hurt, how can you remember to stop and take a deep breath? What would happen if you assumed positive intent?

•

•

•

•

"Darkness cannot drive out darkness;
only light can do that.
Hate cannot drive out hate;
only love can do that."
—Martin Luther King, Jr.

14. Be There When You're There

"Forever is composed of nows."

—Emily Dickinson

You know those perfect summer evenings?

The Goldilocks evenings—not too hot, not too cool. Low humidity. Scarcely a mosquito or gnat to be found. Just right.

The other evening was so beautiful, I decided to sit outside on our deck to watch the sunset. The sky was still light, so I had a few moments to pull out my phone and respond to a friend's text. Then I hopped onto social media and surfed around a bit. I landed on a friend's post from her vacation. She had shared photos of the beautiful scenery of Northern California's rolling wine country and several of a brilliantly colored, painterly sunset. I smiled at the beauty of the photographs—and then jumped, startled into the present moment. I looked up from my phone just in time to see the last of the evening's colors fade beyond the horizon.

I had missed my sunset.

While I had been scanning the pixelated sunset on the six-inch screen in my hand, I had missed the glorious Real Show that had been transforming the sky all around me. The irony of this was not lost on me.

My friend Charmaine had always wanted to see the Blue Angels. If you've ever seen them live, you know it's a powerful, visceral, rock-concert experience. She was so excited she pulled her phone out and started video-taping in an attempt to capture the moment.

"What was I doing?" she lamented later. "Here I was at the event of a lifetime, and I'm seeing it secondhand through my phone. They fly at the *speed of sound*. Did I really think I could record anything that was better than the actual experience?!?"

I've been to concerts, as I'm sure you have, where people have their phones held up, taping the show for two hours straight. Are they really going to watch the replay of the whole event? Seriously, how many times have you actually gone back and re-watched all the video you took at a special event?

People do the same thing at Tim's magic shows. "I don't get it," he shakes his head. "I mean, take a few clips to remember the evening, and post if you want. But you can watch a recording online any time. This is *live* entertainment. It's never the same show twice, and they're missing the chance to be part of something really special and unique."

How often do we miss the real moment because we are distracted by our devices?

There are times when we need to fully experience the moment live and in person and put the phone DOWN.

"Snapping too many pictures could actually harm the brain's ability to retain memories," says Elizabeth Loftus, a psychological-science professor at the University of California, Irvine. You get the photo but kind of lose the memory. She explains that:

* We often are so distracted by the process of taking photos that we miss the moment completely, and/or

* We don't actively remember the moment because we are relying on the technology to capture it instead of our brain

I don't know about you, but I used to have a much better sense of direction before I started relying on my GPS. Same goes for my memory of important phone numbers. Now that I know I can offload responsibility to my phone, I'm at a loss. What if, instead of taking endless photos of a super-special moment, we either:

1. Leave the photography to the professionals, or

2. Limit ourselves to just a few photos, or a video clip or two, but make sure we take the time to fully savor the Real Thing?

It's crazy, I know. Just a thought.

One thing at a time

Being present and living in the moment isn't rocket science. It just takes some concentrated focus on what you're doing at a given moment in time. But in our culture, we pride ourselves on multi-tasking. We confuse busy-ness with accomplishment and wonder why we feel exhausted and empty at the end of the day. The other day I decided to count the number of times I switched gears from one project to the next. I took note of when I jumped from one screen to another on my computer, or when I interrupted a flow to check emails and text messages. I counted nine times that I "multi-tasked." Within one hour.

I felt busy, sure, but when I looked at what I had actually accomplished in that hour, I had to admit, "not so much."

According to Cleveland Clinic's neuropsychologist Cynthia Kubu, PhD, "When we think we're multitasking, most often we aren't doing two things at once . . . we're doing individual actions in rapid succession, or task-switching."

Multi-tasking divides our attention and makes it more difficult to concentrate. According to Dr. Kubu and other really smart people who study this, multi-tasking can make us less efficient and accomplish *less*.

When I concentrate on a particular task without distraction, not only is the result better, but I finish sooner. How about you?

One person at a time

Being present for Our People is as important as being present for a task. One of the simple-but-not-easy things we can do to show someone we care is to give our full attention to them in the present moment. Look at any group of people anywhere, any time, any age. The great percentage of the time, at least one person has their phone out. More often than not, several are glued to their screens. There's a place for it—don't get me wrong. My phone is like an extra appendage that I didn't know I needed but now can't live without. But there is nothing like giving someone the gift of your full attention.

My sister-in-law CJ has a "No Phones at the Table" rule. She will spend hours preparing fabulous meals for us, and, in turn, we put our phones away and savor the meal along with each other's effervescent company. This is an Excellent Rule. If a critical call comes up (which—c'mon, admit it—is rare), we step away from the table. That way, the others can carry on their conversation without waiting in silence, slightly miffed, for the perpetrator to finish the call.

At an annual checkup with my family doctor, I mentioned that my hearing didn't seem quite as bat-like as it used to be. I noticed the difference mostly at home.

"Do you look at your husband when you talk? Or do you have your back turned?" He asked.

Hmmm, point taken. Much of the time I not only have my back turned, we talk to each other from *across the room*. Sometimes we shout to each other from *different rooms* or even *different levels* of the house! Not exactly present.

Here's my new challenge: Look 'em in the eyes

When I'm speaking with someone, I look at the color of their eyes. Not just a cursory glance, and not a creepy, no-blinking stare, either. I concentrate on *see*-ing the color of their eyes. Try this the next time you talk with someone. Give yourself bonus points for details.

* Are their eyes blue?

* Are they really gray-blue with little flecks of aqua here and there?

* Are their eyes brown?

* Are they really warm brown with sparks of toffee and gold?

I get that it depends on your proximity to the other person, and I am not an advocate of invading someone's personal space. *(Along with dirty dishes in the sink, also one of my pet peeves.)* But if you take the time to truly look into another's eyes, you may actually *see* them better. And they will feel *seen.*

I'm working on it. I can truthfully say that, when I put the phone or laundry down or close the laptop and actually look into Tim's eyes, there is a much better connection. I can feel it, and so can he. If the timing's not right, I'm learning to say, "Give me ten minutes to finish this. Then you have my full attention."

Each moment of life is a one-time deal. We don't get to live the same moment twice.

If you're going to be there anyway, then *be* there.

Happiness Practice

Challenge yourself to minimize distractions. Just for a day, an afternoon, an evening:

1. When you are with friends or family, put the phone aside. *(I know, I know. I heard that choking noise. You've GOT this!)* Enjoy what's really happening right there. Right now.

2. The next time you're talking with a loved one, pay attention.
   - ✷ If you're together in person, look into their eyes when you talk. What color are their eyes?
   - ✷ How can you remind yourself to put the phone, book, laptop, paper, distraction away?

> *"If you are depressed, you are living in the past.*
> *If you are anxious, you are living in the future.*
> *If you are at peace, you are living in the present."*
>
> —Lao Tzu

15. Clear the Clutter

"We must take care of our minds because we cannot benefit from beauty when our brains are missing."

—Euripides

My husband loves to go to the dump.

He finds there's something gratifying about loading up all the junk into the SUV, hauling it away, and then sitting back to admire the newly vacated space in the garage. I get it. When I purge my closet of clothes I haven't worn in years or clean out the expired food from the pantry, I feel like I've accomplished something. What is it about the act of de-cluttering that makes us feel more free, more focused? I think there are probably elements of **Control** and **Progress** built into this, but it's more than that. A little extra space, both literally and metaphorically, gives us room to breathe and move about our world more easily.

There are many days where my mind looks like a "before" photo of our garage. Thoughts, worries, and to-do's are stacked up and overflowing like plastic storage bins—jumbled, disorganized, messy. In our current world of 24/7 media and its excessive stimuli, our minds are often restless and scattered. Our world has become loud, with everything shouting for our attention. We can't enjoy a meal at a restaurant or even fill up the gas tank without video screens and noise blaring at us. And yet our best thinking and our best decisions rarely emerge from a distracted, overly busy mind.

Tell the Truth: How often have you made a great decision while lying in bed with your mind racing at 3 a.m.?

Never?

If you're like me, the same thoughts keep reeling and whirling around like clothes in a washing machine. There is a lot of movement and activity, but nothing is going anywhere.

Wouldn't it be better (and way more restful) if we cleared our minds during waking hours, so we can rest at night? Often our best thinking comes while we are driving, or in the shower, or taking a walk, gardening, painting, or at the beach or the lake or the mountains. We make our best decisions when we've cleared the distractions from our minds and can finally hear the voice of our inner sage.

But how do we do that with so much busy-ness in our lives?

Cultivate a Calm Mind

Calmness is a super-power. Cultivate a calm mind, and you can handle anything.

When I was first diagnosed with cancer, my brain switched into 24/7 turbo gear, cranking out endless, scary scenarios. A wise friend suggested I try meditation. I was desperate to dial down the frenetic "what if" soundtrack that was constantly looping in my head. But I was skeptical. I'd tried meditating numerous times, and I always seemed to flunk out. I'd start out so hopeful, following all of the rules:

Sit in a comfortable position.
Feet flat on the floor.
Breathe deeply. . . .

It all seemed simple. But inevitably, my mind would go to one of two places:

1. To my to-do list

2. To sleep

Then my brain would spin over how terrible I was at this. I was stressing out about meditating.

We've all read the research that shows the proven health benefits from meditation, including managing stress and improving concentration and decision-making abilities.

Many highly successful billionaires, including Apple's former CEO Steve Jobs, Oprah Winfrey, and Microsoft co-founder Bill Gates, credit meditation as an important tool that supported their success. Companies like Amazon, Google, and Apple offer meditation classes for employees. But that doesn't mean we can all do it well initially.

Maybe I was trying too hard.

Ultimately, two things helped me quiet down the crazy:

1. **I discovered the Daily Ten.** More on that in a minute.

2. **I gave myself permission to let my thoughts wander.** My brain and I made a deal to not beat me up when my thoughts toddled off aimlessly in some random direction. Instead, I gently brought myself back to focus when I caught myself. It's kind of like being at a train station, objectively observing your thoughts go by like trains. If you find you've boarded one of those train-thoughts and it's taking you down a dark tunnel, just get off at the next station. It's okay. It's just a thought. You can move on.

"Meditation is not about stopping thoughts. A quiet and peaceful mind does not mean an absence of thought. It simply means we are able to observe thinking without getting caught up in it all, without being overwhelmed."

—Andy Puddicombe, Co-Founder of Headspace

The Daily Ten

Whether you call it "meditation," or "centering," or "just sitting quietly," you will not regret investing ten minutes to focus in the morning. My ten minutes looks a bit different from day to day, but here's what works for me:

1. **Play some soft music, take some deep breaths, and focus on three things that you are grateful for.** Let

yourself really savor those three things, not just flit across your consciousness on the way to the next thing.

2. **Send positive energy to someone in your life who needs it.** When I was recovering, people of all religions and races sent me their prayers and energy. One of my colleagues knew someone who knew someone, and, somehow, an entire women's circle in Jamaica was holding me in their hearts and thoughts. I accepted all of that positive intention and felt it like a hug. Regardless of one's beliefs, that much positive energy is like vitamins. It can only help; it certainly can't hurt. And there's so much we don't know.

3. **During those ten morning minutes, set your intentions for the day.** Not so much for what you want to do—that's what your planner is for. But for how you want to *be*. If we are calm and certain, we can handle just about anything. For example, I'll think about what I have planned for the day ahead and ask myself, "How do I need to be to handle this day with grace? Do I need to be extra brave? Forgiving? Playful? Patient?" Somehow, anticipating the emotional state that will be required of me makes it easier to show up that way.

4. **Envision a happy future.** Sometimes, I'll envision myself well into my eighties, healthy and strong, with laugh wrinkles softening my face, a smudge of paint on my chin, and a cute haircut. I'm in a lively sunlit

> room with the blue sky and ocean in the background, savoring the company and love of Tim and My People. I have a dog or two snuggled on my lap or at my feet. Vibrant paintings—many of them of landscapes and people I've met on my travels—are brightening the walls or stacked on the easel, waiting for my brush. My heart is full, grateful for the opportunity to have given back to others even a fraction of the compassion and wisdom others have shared with me. And I am glowing with joy, sparkling with the aliveness and peace of truly *living* my life.

We run from meeting to meeting and thing to thing at such a breakneck speed. I've come to protectively guard those ten minutes each morning as the precious gift that they are.

I make decisions during my Daily Ten.
Stuff happens because of my Daily Ten.

However you invest those ten morning minutes, the day begins with a calm mind and a grateful heart.
Okay, I've made my case.
Are you taking time for yourself each day?

Other ways to clear the mental clutter:

- **Step outside and take a walk.** There is nothing like fresh air and physically moving your body to clear your head.

- **Stand up and stretch.** Seriously, how long have you been sitting? You know you need to get up. Do it.

- **In your company business meetings, make the first item on the agenda one minute of centering.** Whether you use this moment of silence to take a few breaths or stare at the wall in front of you, it's incredible what that infinitesimal investment of time will do to help you shake off the flight or previous meeting and switch gears. I've always found it to be a powerful little reset that leads to a focused mind and a more productive meeting.

- **Yoga, Tai Chi—all good.** Any activity that lets you breathe and focus. Speaking of which:

- **Breathe**—Here's one of my favorites: Breathe to the count of 5. Inhale 1,2,3,4,5. Then hold for 3-5 seconds (don't turn blue) and exhale: 1,2,3,4,5. Do this five times. This is almost foolproof for me for calming my mind to fall back to sleep. The rule is that I have to concentrate on the numbers and can't let my thoughts wander. If I do, I start all over again. It's really boring and much more calming than watching all those sheep fly and frolic about my head.

- **Imagine your Happy Place.** One of my colleagues swears by guided imagery and uses an app (there are many) to help him focus on his favorite place. It could be the sounds and sight of a running stream, or waves rolling gently on the beach. He takes 3 minutes on a break, puts his earbuds in, and escapes for a few minutes, refreshed and ready to come back to the next task at hand.

- **Hug a tree.** Okay, maybe not literally. But there is something about being in nature that immediately centers us. Head to the hills, the park, the ocean, lake, or creek. I have a friend who lives in a condo in Manhattan, overlooking a bodega, a coffee shop, and a hot dog stand. It's awesome. But the best part is her teeny-tiny balcony, which has just enough space for 2 narrow chairs, a bistro table, and a lavish container garden. She has so many flowering plants that you have to contort yourself to reach a chair without knocking over a pot. But it's worth the back sprain just to be out in the air with all that color and greenery. Come to think of it—go ahead and hug that tree.

- **Write.** There's something about clearing your thoughts by putting them in writing in a journal or notebook. There is an immediate feeling of relief: "Ahh, I don't have to keep looping those thoughts over and over. They are right there in that little book if I need them."

- **Doodle, paint, garden, strum that guitar**—as long as the activity doesn't cause additional stress or distraction. The perfect meditative activity takes just enough focus that you can't get caught up in your thoughts, but not so much that it stresses you out even more. Which is why I don't golf.

Watch what you feed your brain

"The more you feed your mind with positive thoughts, the more you can attract great things into your life."

—Roy Bennett

Just as the food we eat impacts our physical health, the conversations we engage in, the news and video we read and watch, all impact our mental health. Are your news and social media habits setting you up for happiness?

How much of the clutter in your brain revolves around bad news? Bad news just sells. Research conducted by the National Academy of Sciences reports that a human bias toward negative news exists largely due to how we've evolved. It's riskier to ignore negative information. . . .

"An ice storm is coming." "There is a saber-tooth tiger in the second cave to the left."

. . . than it is to ignore good news:

"High school grad takes his grandma to the prom." "Man saves baby raccoon."

"Paying attention to negative news," the researchers report, "is generally an effective survival strategy."

Okay, that makes sense. Our brains were designed to protect us. But how do we strike that healthy balance of staying informed without wanting to jump off a ledge? I'm still trying to figure out that tipping point, but sometimes, if the news is getting me down, I've found it best to go on a "news diet" and limit my time online. Observe the news-trains, but don't get carried down a dark tunnel by them. It's too easy to get lulled into that *"Ain't it awful?"* mentality that will suck the joy right out of your day.

3 Good Rules

1. **Start your day with your healthy-happiness routine *before* you jump on the news or social media.** Have you ever grabbed your phone to check the news/social media before even getting out of bed in the morning? Yea, me too. Instead, try starting your day with good habits to set your day up for success. Work out, stretch, savor your Daily Ten—whatever you enjoy doing to start the new day off with a calm mind and a happy heart. In my house, we have a *"No news before Susan's had her coffee"* rule.

2. **No news/social media or business correspondence two hours before bed. Consider a news sabbatical.** There are some well-done daily news summaries and podcasts that you can subscribe to that will give a high-level overview of the news within five to fifteen minutes. This way, you can stay informed without getting sucked in. And watch or read earlier in the day. If the news is making you anxious, don't feel guilty about taking a hiatus. It's your mind, your well-being. You're the

curator of what you allow into your brain. You're the bouncer at the door of your mind. Manage who and what you let in.

Similarly, no business correspondence two hours before bed. I'm a recovering 11 p.m. email-checker. I know, it's a ridiculous habit. There is no way I'm going to able to resolve any business issue at that late hour. Even if I did respond, what have I done? Well, I've just trained the recipient that I work until past 11 p.m. and set the expectation that they will receive a response at all hours of the night. Also, my brain is decidedly not functioning at its best at that late hour. Let me be clear—this is business training and coaching I'm talking about, not emergency brain surgery. If that's your vocation and you're on call, by all means, check in. But otherwise, ask yourself, "Can this wait until tomorrow?"

3. **Take *Action*.** Do something to make a positive difference for someone. Relentless negative news feeds a global sense of helplessness. What good does it do you or our world to freak out and obsess over everything that's wrong? Stop focusing on all the negativity. Instead of asking "What can I possibly do?" Ask "What can I do that's *possible*?" Contribute, create, help, do something that advances the cause. Do something **Kindhearted** for someone. THAT's how we change our world for the good: by taking action—one step, one person, one cause at a time.

Happiness Practice

There is magic that comes with turning over a calendar to a New Year, isn't there? Every January 1, we get a blank slate, a clean canvas, a new opportunity to start fresh. But why should we have to wait a whole year? We have a fresh start with every new day. No matter what we have going on in our lives, each new day has exactly 24 hours. That's 1,440 shiny new minutes. You deserve to have just 10 of those to start the day with a clear head.

1. **The Daily Ten Challenge:** For the next week, commit to a Daily Ten every morning.

   Do this before you start your typical morning routine and get caught up in the day's activities.

   Ask yourself:

   * What are three things I'm grateful for?
     -
     -
     -

   * Who needs some extra love and energy that I can send their way?
     -
     -
     -

- How do I need to *be* today to handle this day with grace and more happiness?
  -
  -
  -

2. The next time a magic moment is unfolding before you, savor the moment live and in person. If you have to take photos, then just take a few. They will be enough to remind you of the moment you actually took time to experience fully.

3. Are you feeling overwhelmed by the news? Consider downloading a podcast or subscribing to a daily email summary. Or perhaps take a news break for a while.

4. What are some other ways that work for you to clear the clutter for a greater sense of calm?
   -
   -
   -

16. Gratitude

Gratitude turns what we have into enough.

—Aesop

What if there were one Happiness Practice that, above all others, was so simple, so powerful, so elegant that it could be used at any moment to overcome life's most destructive emotions?

I used to believe that courage was the antidote to fear.

But I was wrong.

Courage is feeling the fear and stepping up any way.
Gratitude is the antidote to fear.

Get good at exercising this happiness muscle, and you will be armed to deal with any challenge that life throws at you. The key is intentionally **focusing** on what you're grateful for, and **stacking up** these graces high, wide, and deep—even when it seems as if there is absolutely not one, tiny, minuscule hint of a thing that could possibly be good in the situation.

Even in the most Terrible of Days, there is something to be grateful for, if we only decide to stop and look for it, acknowledge it, savor it.

I've often wondered why it seems to take getting smacked in the face with a loss or a great tragedy to bring us together and appreciate what we have. I remember sitting in an unfamiliar church after 9/11, reaching over the pew to hold the hand of the stranger in front of me as we both wept in anguish for our world. We were desperate for solace, for a small gesture of human kindness in the aftermath of that life-altering day that rocked everything we grew up believing.

I was not a member of that church.

I had never sat in that pew.

I had never met this woman.

Yet in that desolate time, we shared a moment of raw vulnerability, of wounded humanity, which bound our souls together completely and instantaneously. I would not recognize that woman on the street today. Yet I am deeply grateful for her in that moment, as I know she was for me.

We can't be happy all the time. There is a time to mourn, to grieve, to fear. It's just as important to our happiness and strong emotional state to fully experience these emotions (Read **Feel It All**). And, there comes a time to move forward, forever changed from the experience. When this time comes, especially in the most devastating times, how can we begin to feel even remotely grateful?

It starts, as always, by making a decision. Decide to feel grateful for something, no matter how small. Focus your attention and *intention* on this one, simple, elegant question:

"What am I grateful for?"

Your brain may stubbornly and justifiably resist: *"Nothing."*

Try again: "Okay, what *could* I be grateful for?"

"Nope. Still nothing."

Try again.

And again.

Regardless of the challenge you are experiencing, eventually, your brain can't help but respond. After all, it's the most miraculous problem-solving instrument ever created, and you just lobbed it a world-class problem:

"What am I grateful for?"

"I don't have to do this alone."

"They caught the tumor early."

"I have the courage to leave him/her and move on with my life."

"I have the skills. I can get another job."

"I am so grateful I had her/him in my life as long as I did."

Practicing gratefulness works to help ease life's Big Problems. But where we build this muscle is in finding the small moments we can be grateful for in our typical, moving-through-life days.

The small stuff is the big stuff.

I've kept journals on and off throughout my life. But I started being very intentional about my gratefulness journal when I was recovering from spine cancer. My challenge to myself was to come up with three things I was grateful for every day. Sometimes I had to think long and hard. Sometimes I had to be creative. Inevitably, the answers came to me:

1. I'm grateful for a really great book on my reader.

2. I'm grateful for my neighbor's homemade turkey noodle soup.

3. I'm grateful for the way Tim props the pillows around me to try to make me comfortable before he kisses me goodnight.

This little game I played, which felt forced at first, eventually became a cherished ritual of my day. It still is. And the funny thing about **focus** is that *we get what we focus on*. The more I focused on insignificant little things I was even just slightly grateful for, the more momentum I gained, the easier it was to build the list, the more grateful I felt, and the happier I became. I often found myself in tears, humbled from all of the many acts of kindness from people who showed up for me when I most needed them. I poured my gratefulness into a love letter to my friends and family, which barely began to nudge at the deep sense of gratitude that I felt.

The happy people I know *all* focus on mastering the practice of gratitude. Even now, as I climb under the covers at night, tired or uninspired, I'll open the journal on my nightstand and jot down three things that I'm grateful for and close the book. Or I'll lie quietly in those few moments before sleep and savor those three moments in my memory. It *always* makes me happier.

Here are some examples of entries from my gratefulness journal:

I'm grateful for:

1. The first, really ripe, really red strawberries of the season from the farmer's market stand
2. Long, hot showers
3. Lavender shower foam

1. The way Elsie walks around to my side of the bed in the morning and lays her head next to mine, willing me to wake up and scratch her silky ears
2. Wine delivery service
3. My dad called me back after we hung up to tell me he forgot to say, "I love you"

1. Waking up to birdsong
2. And going to sleep to frog-song. Which, by the way, is very, very LOUD
3. Come to think of it—songs. Music moves me

1. Reconnecting with my college roommate and bridesmaid, Maria
2. The first bite of a great slice of pizza
3. A real hug-like-you-mean-it hug

And here are a few lists from My People:

1. My tulips are popping up. And they've multiplied! I planted 40 bulbs and have 54 flowers
2. My son came and visited over dinner
3. We took a nice walk through the park

1. Sticking those little spring leaf "helicopters" on my son's nose. Okay, and on mine, too
2. Multi-colored Post-It notes
3. Opening up a fresh bag of coffee

1. The way my daughter throws her head back and belly laughs
2. How my cat walks over my knees and teases my nose with her tail while I'm on video calls
3. Listening to rain on the roof. And knowing I can sleep in because it's Saturday

Gratitude is the simplest, yet most powerful practice we can do to consistently find and have more joy in life.

"Sometimes the smallest things take up the most room in your heart."

—Christopher Robinson

Happiness Practice

* What are three things that you are grateful for right now?
  1.
  2.
  3.

* As you go to bed at night, between flossing and brushing, or kissing your loved ones goodnight, or saying your prayers, or reflecting on the day—whatever your night time routine is, add this one simple question:

  What are three things that I'm grateful for today?
  1.
  2.
  3.

A Letter of Gratitude to My People

Caringbridge.com's vision is that no one go through a health journey alone. I am deeply grateful for this brilliant, innovative non-profit which allows you to create a free website to communicate with loved ones without making dozens of emotional and time-consuming phone calls or sending numerous emails, allowing caregivers and patients more time, meaningful connections, and greater levels of peace.

Dear Loved Ones,

Today was another milestone since my surgery, and I celebrated by getting fired. Twice.

Once by my Physical Therapist who, after teaching me some stretches to build my muscles back up and learning that I am walking 1.5–2 miles a day, rolled her eyes and said, "You don't need me." And then by my visiting nurse who, for the first time, was able to sit with me at the table (because I can sit now!) and is "amazed and thrilled" by my recovery.

So, as of this week, there are no more tubes, drains, stitches, staples, or other paraphernalia attached to me—just me! The extreme movement restrictions were lifted. And, now my job is to heal fully and not push it. I've been given strict instructions by my surgeon—and Tim—to rest, sit, lie down, stay—whenever I need to and to take it slowly. I'm still waiting for my system to recover from the nerve "shock" that typically accompanies this procedure, and that will just take time. I know—patience, patience. Blah blah blah . . .

So, here is the love-letter portion of this update. And there go my eyes again, welling up just thinking of your many kindnesses these last months. My emotions seem to be very close to the surface these days. There is simply no combination of words to thank you. No words. But you have touched my heart and soul, and I will try. So here goes. . . .

Thank you:

For the many prayers, emails, texts, and phone calls that make me laugh or offered words of encouragement and hope. And for just listening. And for knowing when to talk about anything else.

To all of you who sat in the chairs next to me while I lay on my left side in the hospital bed in our living room—talking, laughing, listening, or just sitting in silence with me, reading our respective books and readers.

For throwing a load of laundry in, or emptying the dishwasher, running errands or texting me "I'm at Target. Can I pick up anything for you?" to give Tim a little break.

To my colleagues at work who stepped in and kept things going while I couldn't.

To the friends who, knowing we couldn't travel home for Thanksgiving, swooped in with a feast with all the trimmings, and left the kitchen spotless when they left.

For bringing Christmas to our home—decorating the tree and the mantle and leaving me with tears in my eyes (again!) to marvel at the twinkly, festive beauty and magic of it all.

For the chefs and foodies who whipped up or went out of your way to pick up amazing food—chicken pot pies, brownies, miracle peanut butter protein balls, Graul's chicken salad, homemade soup, chicken BBQ, and SO much more . . . !

To not just a few of you, but to Every Single One of You who, without exception, shunned the nearby chairs to stand in solidarity with me at the kitchen island for dinner—because you knew I couldn't sit.

For babysitting (and spoiling!) our sweet greyhound, Elsie, for many days and nights—so Tim could be with me at the hospital and get me home and past that "fragile" point.

For the many beautiful cards, some of which came from people I don't even know. But they took the time to send them because you mean so much to them, and they know how much I mean to you.

For the gorgeous bouquets that brightened up our home and my spirits. And the thoughtful care packages with fresh fruit, herbal tea, cozy socks, good reads, chocolate, soft blankets.

For checking in on Tim to make sure he was okay. I knew he was Magic from the moment we met, but I am perpetually blown away by his attention and care for me, and your care for him.

Most of all, thank you for reminding me that, through this journey, I was and still am—me, Susan. Without undermining the seriousness of this, you didn't let me take myself too seriously. You helped me stay strong-hearted and brave when I felt weak, and reminded me of the best in me when I felt the worst. For every moment I felt down,

there were countless more when I felt uplifted and grateful,
and supremely blessed.

I've been lucky enough to have been loved my whole life, since the day I was born. Yet I don't know that I've ever felt more loved than I do now.

Thank you,
Susan

17. Control

"Worrying does not empty tomorrow of its troubles.
It empties today of its strength."
—Corrie Ten Boom

I never realized just how critical having a sense of control was to me until I had none.

Lying in that hospital bed in the Intensive Care Unit, connected to wires, pumps and tubes, I felt humbled, vulnerable, and, for the first time in my life, completely at the mercy of others. Until then, I truly thought I was in control. I had been taught at a young age that, if I focused my talents and energy, worked hard, and did the right thing, I would get results. And in many respects, that was true.

- Apply yourself to school = Get good grades

- Eat the right portions of nutritious foods, exercise regularly, make healthy lifestyle choices = Build a fit and healthy body

- Never stop learning and growing = Become more resourceful and insightful

- Work hard and smart, and bring constant value = Achieve success and get results

- Give more than is expected and do the right thing= Enjoy a wonderful life and sleep soundly at night

This desire for certainty and control is wired into us as human beings. Again, science tells us this built-in need is probably a survival mechanism. If we have control, we can mitigate risk, protect ourselves and our loved ones, and forge the path forward that we want. Yet sometimes, *Something Happens* that scrambles the formula as we know it, leaving us feeling unmoored and unhinged from what was our reality. For me, that was a cancer diagnosis. *Wait a minute! The women in my family live well into their 80s, 90s, and beyond. I'm the picture of health. I eat right. I win fitness competitions, for heaven's sake. This is not how the story is supposed to go. Someone wake me up NOW!*

In the first weeks after the diagnosis, I experienced sudden, sporadic episodes of tightness in my chest, erratic heartbeat, shallow breathing. I know now that these were anxiety attacks, the result of my whole, controlled worldview being cataclysmically turned inside out. But at the time, I was shocked when, after describing the physical sensations to my doctor, he said, "Well, of course. You're having a panic attack."

He might as well been talking to me in Njerep. (*An obscure language spoken by only four people in the world. Look it up, it's fascinating. . . .*) That's how foreign the idea of having a panic attack felt to me. Panic attacks, like cancer, happened to *other* people, not me. Until they did.

At the heart of feelings of anxiety, or plain, old-fashioned stress, is the feeling of a loss of control. And control is an illusion that we continue to chase.

If things are feeling a bit out of control, we tend to want to control the things that we can. Sometimes, it (temporarily) helps to do something we *can* control to stop us from freaking out about all the things we can't. To this day, things can be spinning out of control, and I will stop what I'm doing to put the dishes away. Even as I write this, there is mail piled up on the kitchen island and clothes overflowing the laundry hamper, but, gosh darn it, my kitchen sink is empty and sparkling clean!

It makes me feel better.

That's a more positive consequence of a control issue. It's much more damaging when we try to get our footing back by controlling the *people* around us. How does that work out?

There are plenty of highly trained therapists helping people deal with their control issues. In my experience, it comes down to setting yourself up for success. To do this, we need to pay attention to the Sweet Spot, that intersection of:

1. What matters most to us *and*

2. What we can actually control

I debated whether to start and end this chapter with this graphic and the words,

"Nuff Said."

We **know** this, right? We know we can't control so much of what happens in our lives.

So why do we continue to worry, and spin, and torture ourselves over things we cannot control? There has to be a better way. Maybe even three.

3 Better Ways

Here are three ways to set you up for success when it comes to control:

1. **Keep things in perspective.** Ask yourself, "Does it matter? Is it really important?" If not—*let it go.*

   This falls under the category of "Don't sweat the small stuff." Okay, it drives me a little nuts that Tim leaves papers all over the place. And I know it annoys him that I always seem to find "one more thing" that needs to be done as we are all set to walk out the front door. But in the big picture, these things don't matter. Keep it all in perspective.

Take a breath. Let it go. Repeat.

2. **We can't always control the events that happen to us. But we *can* take action to set ourselves up for success.**

   There is nothing like a plan of action to help us feel like we have regained some semblance of control. Remember the Power of **Progress**? One step at a time.

After my diagnosis, as soon as I scheduled a consultation with the recommended neurosurgeon, I felt a huge sense of relief. As soon as Tim and I met with him and we had a plan of action, I felt even better. The tumor was still there, exactly where it had been, but now we had a step-by-step plan. Making the appointment, setting a course of action—these were actionable steps I could control, in a sea of uncontrollable. All progress starts with that first, intentional step. Taking steps we *can* control helps us regain our sense of balance and equilibrium, even in an uncontrollable, uncertain situation.

* Let's say you're catching a flight to a business meeting. You can't control the flight being delayed. But you *can* control getting to the airport early so that you're not

white knuckled and stressed about getting to your gate on time.

* You can't control someone else's reaction to unwelcome news, but you *can* communicate and listen with compassion and empathy.

* You can't control a prospective employer's decision to hire you or a client's decision to buy from you, but you *can* prepare and present your value in a confident, credible, and authentic manner.

* You can't control every health diagnosis, but you can do the right things to take care of yourself physically, mentally, and emotionally, and have a plan of action if things do go awry.

* You can't control how someone else feels about you, but you can always control how *you* feel about yourself.

And then, there's this:

3. **We can't always control the events that happen to us. But we can *always* control the *meaning* we give these events.**

Next chapter, please. Read on. . . .

Happiness Practice

- What is something that is feeling a little (or a lot) out of control right now?

- In the big scheme of things, is it important? Does it matter to you? Why or why not?

- What is one thing you *can* do to set yourself up for success?

- What's another?

Write this all down. And re-read **Progress and Stack Life in Your Favor.**

18. Meaning

"The problem is not the problem.
The problem is your attitude about the problem."
—Captain Jack Sparrow

How is it that two people can experience the exact same event and each take a completely different meaning from it?

I remember being led into the examination room at my doctor's office by his assistant, Fran. She had recovered from breast cancer while I was recovering from spine cancer, and we immediately bonded over our shared-ish experience. She was happily, fully recovered from the chemo, and I had witnessed her hairstyle progression from head turban to Audrey Hepburn pixie cut, to today's swingy, shoulder-length bob.

"You look great," I said, sincerely. "How are you doing?"

She hesitated a moment before answering. "Okay, I guess," she shrugged. "I'm healthy, but I still can't believe that my body did this to me."

"I can't believe my body did this to me."

Wait, what??

Her comment made me pause. She meant the cancer, of course. In that moment, it struck me that the meaning she took from her experience, or one of the meanings, was that her body had turned against her, as if the cells of her own body had conspired to intentionally do this *to* her.

Clearly, your own body turned against you has to be the most invasive adversary one can have. But how must that mindset, that meaning—"body turned against me"—impact the way she goes about her days? Even though she was recovered and healthy again, she was obviously still carrying a heavy emotional burden that slumped her shoulders and drew her pretty face into a frown at the very thought.

She had a right to feel that way, of course, or any other way she chose to feel, for that matter. There are experiences in our lives that turn our world upside down and cause us to ask *WHY? And Why ME?* I have certainly done my share of asking. Yet the meaning I took from the experience I had with cancer was somehow different. Oh, it sucked—don't get me wrong. But I never once *blamed* my body for giving me cancer. My body is my ally, not my enemy.

It's been said that everything in life happens for a reason. I don't know that I believe that. I did nothing to cause cancer, certainly nothing to deserve it. Sometimes stuff just happens. There are certain laws of physics and gravity and biology. Cars cross the yellow line. Trees fall. Cells divide.

Neither of us was right *or* wrong. But each of us was making a *decision,* consciously or unconsciously, about the meaning we gave a similar, rotten experience. And that decision, that *meaning,* very directly impacted our mindset and subsequent behavior.

I thought about that for a while as I swung my bare feet above the linoleum floor and waited on the exam table in my paper robe. I heard a light rap at the door.

"How are you doing?" my neurosurgeon asked as he walked into the room with a smile.

"Fantastic!" I said, maybe a little too enthusiastically, but meaning it, nonetheless.

I am blown away by how much my body went through and how well it recovered. With more than 30 trillion cells, a heart that beats, and lungs that breathe all day and all night without my giving them a passing thought—my body is freakin' miraculous! THAT is the meaning I'm choosing to take from this.

It's not the event that controls our emotions. It's the meaning we give it.

Quick, without thinking about it too much, finish this sentence with the first word that pops into your brain:

1. Life is _____.

* How did you answer the question?

* How would someone who views life as a "gift" react to events, as opposed to one who views life as a "struggle"? What about Life is . . . a blessing? Or Life is . . . a challenge? Or Life is . . . a blast?

* Think of the meaning behind your response. It's an interesting little glimpse into your worldview—at the moment, anyway.

It's NOT the situation or events in life that control our emotions. It's what we tell ourselves about the events. Are you really going to let the weather, an offhand comment, or the number on the scale determine your level of happiness for the day? In this, as in all situations, we have a choice about how we feel. It all starts with the *meaning* we give things.

We instantaneously attach meanings to all kinds of events that happen in our lives. But our brains work so fast, we often don't stop to assess how we got there. We just know that the boss walked by, and now we're grumpy, or anxious, or happy, or curious—depending on the meaning we attach to "the boss" at that particular moment. Our brains go through a rapid-fire process when attaching meanings, and we often live with the consequences of those meanings for years.

Every day, we read about road rage ending tragically. What causes someone to react so violently when another driver cuts them off, while others just roll their eyes and carry on? It's important to think about the meanings we give things, as they affect all of our emotions, including happiness. And it's these emotions that impact our behavior. Our behavior, in turn, triggers others to make assumptions about what our behavior means, and behave accordingly. It's an interesting cycle, often filled with misinterpretations, misperceptions, and miscommunications, but it is a real thing.

To see how this works, let's break down this process that our brains go through into its three components:

Event: Something happens. We have no control over it.

Meaning: We instantaneously ask ourselves: What does this *mean*? Here, we *have* control. What meaning do we give this? What else could it mean? Could we choose to believe a different, more positive meaning?

Behavior: This choice we make about meaning affects our behavior, which, in turn, affects the behavior of those around us.

Let me give you an example:

I remember burning up over a terse "howler" email from a colleague, screaming at me in ALL CAPS at 11:15 p.m. It felt harsh and unfair. I stewed over it and lost several hours of sleep that night. When I asked him about it the next morning, he sheepishly admitted, "Geez, sorry. I was exhausted so my message was short. And I have a new computer and the caps lock must have been on."

I let a poor choice of meaning rob me of a good night's sleep! *And what was I doing checking business email at 11:15 p.m., anyway?!* But that's another chapter . . . .

Event: EMAIL IN ALL CAPS

Meaning: My colleague is shouting at me!

Behavior: Fuming and tossing all night

Here's another example:

Years ago, on a cruise, Tim and I met two sisters who were traveling together—Harriett and Carla. Harriett was on-board to teach Tai Chi to the passengers. Carla came along for the ride because, you know, *who wouldn't?* We loved meeting up with them for dinner. Not only did we enjoy their company, we couldn't wait to see the impromptu fashion show they put on at our table every evening. Harriett and Carla had style, and we never knew what to expect.

* One evening, they both showed up wearing elephant-print parachute pants with coordinating T-shirts.

* Another time, it was silky sarongs with embroidered tropical birds and flowers.

* Then there was the time they both walked in wearing black, high-neck dresses. They looked sophisticated and perfectly elegant. But, frankly, we were a little disappointed, given the colorful standard they had set on previous evenings.

And then, they turned around. . . .

There, emblazoned across their shoulders, was a vibrant splash of mango-eating monkeys. That ensemble was definitely the Fan Favorite.

And to think that all of that fun would never have happened if the cruise line hadn't lost Carla's and Harriet's luggage.

Wait, scratch that. Cruise lines and airlines lose luggage all the time, and many people would choose a different meaning and react *very* differently than our resident fashion icons did.

Carla and Harriet could have been angry and upset about their lost luggage. They could have whined and ranted and let that one "lost luggage" event ruin their whole vacation. They might have made such a fuss that they ruined our evening as well. But instead, Carla and Harriet *decided* that they were going to see just how much fun they could have, and just how creative they could be with a $10 fashion budget in each port of call. And guess what? They had a blast doing it. And so did we.

Event: Lost luggage
Meaning they chose: "Well, we can't do anything about this. We might as well have some fun with this until our luggage meets up with us."
Behavior: Fashion show on a budget

Let's look at a few more examples. Does this one look familiar? Okay, not for you, of course, but maybe you KNOW someone who reacts like this. . . .

Event: It's raining, you're caught in traffic, and now you're 20 minutes late for work.
Meaning: *What meaning will you choose to give this?* The stupid weather made me late!
Behavior: Snap at a colleague, or mess up the presentation, have a terrible day—because the *weather and traffic made me late*!

Event: Your friend is late meeting you at the restaurant. They haven't called or texted.

Meaning: *What meaning will you choose to give this? Some options:*

- Maybe they got caught in traffic.
- Maybe they forgot.
- They are always late to meet me. They are disrespecting me and my time!
- Oh, no! What if they were in an accident?!
- They're probably just running a little late.

Behavior: Depending upon the meaning you give this, you're going to react differently, aren't you? If you believe your friend is disrespecting you and could have called, then you will respond very differently than if you believe they are tied up in traffic—or worse, were in an accident. In one case, you may greet them with a cold shoulder and a terse word or two. In another case, a grateful and relieved hug.

How about this?

Event: A trusted friend or loved one lashes out at you. It's unwarranted, and it's hurtful.

Meaning: *What meaning will you choose to give this?*

- "That was out of line. She has no right to say that to me." OR
- "Wow. She is under a ton of stress right now with work. I'm going to give her a pass on that one and not take it personally."

Behavior: It will be different again, depending upon the meaning you give the situation, right? In the first instance, you could lash back with a counterattack, which only triggers and escalates the tension. Or, you could take a breath, empathize, and say something like, "I know you're under a lot of stress right now. And I know you didn't mean that. What's going on?"

SAC IT!

Okay, so how do we go about making better, more conscious choices about the meanings we give to the events in our lives, for happier outcomes?

There is a skill to this practice, and, once again, it's very simple. And not easy. I know, I know. It's a theme.

When an event occurs that triggers a negative reaction, SAC it.

STOP. Take a deep breath before reacting reflexively.
Ask yourself, "What does this mean?" "Is it true?" "What else could this mean?"
Choose the most empowering meaning, and act accordingly.

Here's an example of how this works:

Event: You receive a text from a friend: "Don't you EVER check your text messages??!!"
STOP. Take a breath.
Ask: What could this mean? *"She's being rude, impatient."* What ELSE could this mean?

Choose: A better meaning: *"She must have something urgent on her mind that needs immediate attention. I'll call her directly."*

Event: An old friend who lives out of state calls to coordinate a time to visit with you. You rearrange your schedule several times to accommodate his schedule. It is now the third time he has called to cancel the day before your scheduled date, without explanation. GO:

STOP. Take a breath.
ASK: What does this mean? *"He doesn't value my time."* What else could it mean?
Choose: *"There must be something really critical going on in his life to keep shifting our visit. I'll give him the benefit of the doubt."*

BONUS: Assume Positive Intent

When in doubt, always assume positive intent, especially when it comes to those you love most. Even if you're *right*, choosing to believe a negative meaning often leads to raised voices and verbal attacks. And that's just toxic and damaging.

We give meanings to events that happened years ago and often carry around the weight and stress of these choices for *years*. Here's an example of how choosing a more positive meaning can impact our lives for decades.

My friend Eileen is one of the brightest, most well-adjusted, emotionally stable people I know. Looking at her and the life that she's built for herself and her family, you'd never guess that she had a very challenging childhood. The oldest of five, Eileen grew up taking care of her four younger siblings at the ripe old age of ten. Her father had abandoned the family. Her mother, the sole adult caretaker, had severe physical disabilities and suffered from extreme depression.

Eileen doesn't talk about it much, because she chooses not to **focus** on the negative.

- But she remembers the times she had to knock on the neighbors' doors to beg for food. Often, there was nothing to eat in their house because their mom couldn't get out of bed to go to the grocery store.

- She remembers wearing hand-me-down clothes from strangers, donated from the local church.

- She remembers the winter nights they all huddled together in bed, wrapped in layers of clothing, because the electricity bill hadn't been paid, and the heat had been shut off.

What meaning could she have pulled from her childhood?

1. She could have chosen to believe that nothing in life is fair.

2. She might have blamed every tough break or bad situation in her life on the fact (event) that she had a difficult childhood.

3. She could have carried the weight of the injustices of her childhood for her entire life, acting out as a "victim," perpetuating a cycle of poverty, and maybe even crime.

She could have believed all of these things or worse, and we would shake our heads with understanding and pity. But Eileen and her siblings took a different meaning from their childhood. The meaning they *decided* to take away was, "If we stick together, we'll make it together."

Instead of blaming their childhood and feeling like victims of circumstances they couldn't control, they focused on what they *could* control. They used their situation as fuel to propel them forward in life. They had each other's backs. They took jobs mowing the lawn, babysitting, and, later, working at restaurants and mechanic shops. They pooled their paychecks, resources and talents. They supported each other and, together, applied for scholarships and grants to go to university. All five took action, got educated, worked hard, and today are raising close-knit families with great values and work ethics. They enjoy being together, giving back, and making a positive difference in the lives of others who are less fortunate.

Event: Growing up in a broken home
Meaning she chose: "Family sticks together. Together we can make it."
Behavior: Support and encourage each other to strive for a better life, despite current difficulties

Whether they realized it or not, Eileen and her siblings were SAC-ing it.

Stop: Take a breath
Ask: What does this mean? *Am I just unlucky? This is my lot in life. I have no control. The world is out to get me!*
Choose: A better meaning: *Family sticks together. Together, we can make it.* We can take control and create wonderful lives—*despite* and *because* of our challenging childhood.

It's not the event that controls our emotions; it's the meaning we give it. We don't always get to control the events and situations in our lives. But we *always* get to control the meaning we give things.

Happiness Practice

- What is an event or situation that has happened that is bothering you? *Write it down.*
  -
  -
  -
  -
  -

- What meaning do you have to give this event in order to feel so irked? *You know the drill. Write it down.*
  -
  -
  -
  -
  -

- Choose: What else might it mean? Is there another possible option that is more favorable? One that will incite a more positive response?
  -
  -
  -
  -
  -

- What can you do to act on this better response? How can you SAC it?
  -
  -
  -
  -

Stop—take a breath
Ask *What does this mean?*
Choose a better meaning

- What if you gave someone the benefit of the doubt? What meaning would you need to believe about them or the situation? How would you respond then?
  -
  -
  -
  -

"My life has been full of tragedies, most of which never actually happened."

—Mark Twain

19. Identity

"Life isn't about finding yourself.
Life is about creating yourself."
—George Bernard Shaw

Our sense of identity, or how we perceive ourselves, is one of the strongest forces that shapes our behavior, our sense of self-worth, our level of happiness. Our self-perception controls how we see ourselves, how we interact with those around us, and how others respond to us.

For example:

* If you see yourself as a "vegan," as opposed to a "meat-lover," you are going to make very different choices about what you eat.

* If you see yourself as an "athlete," you are going to move about the world differently than if you see yourself as "uncoordinated."

* If you see yourself as "funny," you are going to interact with people differently than if you see yourself as "serious."

Hipster, geek, feminist, philanthropist, outspoken, diplomatic, rebel, gay, straight, smoker, non-smoker, skeptic, optimist, good-in-a-crisis, drama queen. . . . All of these "labels" we use, either consciously or subconsciously, are the shorthand we use to communicate to ourselves and the world about who we are.

Some of these labels are rooted in the genetic hand we were dealt as well as in our culture, environment, and upbringing, societal norms, and decisions we've made. I'm a wife. I'm a husband. I'm a daughter, son, mom, dad, black, white, attorney, doctor, etc. But many of these labels that we use to describe our own identity are self-imposed. In many cases, we've been carrying old labels from our past that someone else gave us. Somehow, we allow these old labels to hang around and define us well past their expiration date.

The question is: Are these labels serving you?

Is acting consistent with this identity making you happy? Or do you need to reboot and download a more empowering, updated version?

I have a massage therapist who is fabulous at her profession. She knew my history with cancer. She knew that I couldn't lie on my back for an extended period of time because of the missing vertebrae. She also knew that I had neck pain. So, the first time I was healed enough to see her after I shattered my shoulder, she gasped and blurted out, "You are a MESS!"

Now, she may have intended it to be empathetic or funny. But I chose a more negative **meaning,** and heard it in a judgy, non-empathetic, un-funny way. The more I tried to relax, the more her comment bugged me. As the soothing spa music chimed on in the background, I erupted.

"I am NOT a mess. I am a ***Fucking WARRIOR!!!***"

Whoa. I know.

I'm not proud of that moment. And she wasn't exactly wrong. When you stack up those injuries, it's easy to jump to the conclusion she came to. Except that's not how I see myself. My identity, my self-perception, is that my body is incredibly strong and resilient, to have carried me around the world, to have recovered from two very serious surgeries within four months of each other. To have fought back to the point where I could work out, and walk, and paint, and sit on a freakin' spin bike and exercise my ass off again—*without* a tailbone and a couple of vertebrae.

Regardless of who was right, or wrong, or anything in between, think about this:

How would one who is a "mess" go through life, as opposed to one who sees herself as an "F-ing warrior"?

Don't get me wrong, there are plenty of moments when I feel the mess, but it's the *situation* that's a mess, not *me.* Do you see the difference?

We both apologized that day, and we're okay. But the moment had me thinking about what was behind my visceral reaction and the power of identity.

One of my friends was experiencing bouts of unexplained dizziness and sought out testing to determine the cause.

MRIs, appointments with Ear, Nose, and Throat specialists, cardiologists, you name it. Finally, her doctor sent her to a vertigo specialist. When she told him her medical history, she explained that the last time she had experienced bouts of dizziness was when she was first diagnosed with breast cancer, more than ten years ago.

"Ahh, well it's obvious then, isn't it?" he concluded loftily. "That's what's causing your current condition. You are a **Panic Attack Person**."

"You know," she told me over coffee later that week, "I tried that on for size. At first, I was mad. But then I got to thinking, what if he was right? Could I actually *be* a Panic Attack Person?"

This friend happens to be one of the coolest, calmest people I know. She has walked through fire with a smile on her face many times throughout her life. What was concerning is that this *stranger,* despite his credentials, was causing her to question herself, her own identity. Now, *I* was mad!

"You're right," she said. "He doesn't know me. Yes, I've had panic attacks, but that doesn't make me a Panic Attack *Person*. What the heck is a 'Panic Attack Person' anyway?"

As it turned out, her dizziness was caused by an inner-ear issue which resolved itself. But what if she had stopped there and started believing this guy? What could that belief of herself have done to the quality of her life? Or her ability to manage stressful times in the future?

**We can't let other people tell us who we are.
We have to decide that for ourselves.**

As human beings, we have access to a full range of emotions and experiences. But we are not our emotions. Emotions, like experiences, are temporary. They are not who we ARE.

Have you ever felt angry?

Does that mean you are an *Angry Person*?

Of course not. Not unless you see yourself that way.

WARNING: Be careful of the labels you use for yourself. We tend to act, consciously or unconsciously, in a way that reinforces our own self-beliefs.

There are labels I use for myself that I want to keep: optimist, artist, writer, entrepreneur, friend, creative, listener, explorer, coach, animal-rescuer, nature-lover. . . . But there are labels that don't serve as well.

Here's the supercool thing:

Change your label—Change your behavior—Change your life.

Growing up, I was a "Good Girl." I was a pleaser who worked hard to excel in school and did everything in my power to make my parents proud and my friends want to hang out with me. That served me well . . . up to a point.

As a "Good Girl," I rarely ruffled feathers or rocked the boat. I played it safe and stayed in my comfort zone. I frequently swallowed my voice to avoid conflict or risk disapproval. And

I often took my cues from the people around me, rather than listen to my own inner voice.

So, years ago, I decided: *Good Girl's Gotta Go.*

She was no longer serving me and the dreams I had for my life. If I was going to attract a partner and friends who were living their lives at a higher level, build a business, travel the world, put my best, bravest self out there to make a positive difference, then I was going to have to stretch myself in bigger ways. And to do that, I needed an identity upgrade. So, I traded Good Girl in for a new identity, "Hot Rocket!" Where Good Girl was accommodating, Hot Rocket! is compassionate, but is also bold and courageous, and takes *action.* If I'm on-fire excited and also a little scared, I must be doing it right.

Sometimes I felt like I was faking it. Sometimes I still do. But even when I had to "act as if," I kept practicing. I continually asked myself, "What would my braver self do in this situation?" "How would Hot Rocket! handle this?" And eventually, I *became* that person.

In order to help my clients, I have to speak tough truths to leaders in a way that they can hear, and also inspire and arm them with tools to take action. I would never have been able to do this as the "Good Girl."

I would have never been able to deal with cancer (little c) or write this book as "Good Girl." But, as Hot Rocket!? Well, the sky is the limit.

I'm still *practice*-ing, and sometimes I blow it. But I *know* that every time I show the courage to do that big thing that scares me at the risk of stretching myself outside my comfort zone, life wildly rewards me for it.

- So, are you conforming to an identity that no longer serves you?
- Are you playing it small or safe?
- Is this getting in the way of your happiness and your dreams?

Then let's create a new identity that represents an even better version of your already fabulous self.

Happiness Practice

- What labels do you use for yourself? Write down at least six. Make sure to include self-labels that you can change if you want to.

1.

2.

3.

4.

5.

6.

- Which of these labels serve you and make you happy? These are the ones you want to keep.
  -
  -
  -
  -
  -

✷ What behaviors do you demonstrate consistently to exemplify this label/identity?

-
-
-
-
-

✷ Which labels are no longer serving you?

-
-
-
-
-

✷ What behaviors do you demonstrate consistently to exemplify this behavior?

-
-
-
-
-

✷ What new, more-empowering labels/identity can you take on to kick that old disempowering identity to the curb?

-
-
-
-
-

* What actions and behaviors will you demonstrate to support this identity upgrade?
    -
    -
    -
    -
    -

20. Savor the Moments

"Some days I wish I could go back in life.
Not to change anything, but to feel a few things twice."
—Unknown, but I wish I'd said it.

In the *Harry Potter* series, there is a magical mirror powerful enough to have earned its own name, "Erised." This legendary mirror showed you your heart's greatest *desire*—which is "Erised" spelled backwards. (*Clever, huh?*) If you weren't careful, it would hold you transfixed, lost in its charm for all of eternity.

We have our own Erised, only it's not at all ominous. On the table by our front door is an electronic photo frame that, like that magical mirror, has an almost magnetic ability to stop us in our tracks as we are walking out the door. On many occasions, it has delayed our walks to the point where our dogs, all leashed up and ready to go, resign themselves with a sigh and lie down on the carpet to wait us out.

Tim is a wonderful photographer and, even better, makes the time to continually update the SD card, so we have decades of photos on that frame. There are the Main Events, of course—weddings and anniversaries, travels, and holidays. There are lots of photos with friends and family, usually accompanied by good food and wine. And there are photos of loved ones, now gone, which always bring about a bittersweet pause.

There are also photos that capture small moments that might otherwise be forgotten in the busy-ness of life.

1. There is the photo of the time we waited a very long time in a very long line in rented pants to have our photograph taken at the Grand Palace in Thailand, only to be photo-bombed by a young Chinese man. Apparently, in Asia, it's good luck to be photographed with two blondes. *"Xie Xie!"*

2. There is a photo of the men in my family proudly posing with their new Christmas presents over their jeans, the year my mom decided it was a good idea to get them all neon-colored boxer shorts.

3. Or, the one from our Thanksgiving photo shoot, when Tim tried out the "continuous shooting" function on his new camera. By rapid-fire shot #7, we had picked up the camera's rhythm, ditched our standard photo-op smiles, and were hamming it up for the camera with muscle poses, peace signs, and wrestling holds.

4. And, because Tim is the *Keeper of the Frame,* there is the less-than-flattering one of me, mildly passed out in the middle of the living room floor, our dog's head on my stomach, surrounded by tufts of obliterated dog toy.

> Unwashed dinner plates and an (empty) wine bottle are visible in the background.

Life is made of moments.

Even in the most mundane of days, providence can surprise and delight us with a moment that is so pure, so full of grace, so magical, that it makes us pause and breathe and remember how wonderful it is to be alive. These moments, of course, are happening around us, more often than we notice.

How often do these wonderful memories, these moments of grace, flit across our consciousness, only to be quickly replaced by the to-do list in our head, the mission we were set on accomplishing before we were so momentarily awestruck?

What if we were to savor these moments and memories, truly let all of our senses enjoy them for a moment or two, before we moved on with our day?

My grandfather was one of the most powerful influences in my young life. He was almost 70 when I was born, so I always remember him being older, although he never seemed *old*. He woke up slowly, which boded well for my brothers and me when we heard him making his way to the one bathroom in the cottage where we spent our summers together. If we timed it right, we could zip into the bathroom, do our business, brush our teeth, and hop back into bed while he was still greeting himself and the new day with a hearty "Good Morning, Charlie!" Out of all of the qualities I adored about him—his kindness, his spark, his gentle spirit, his patience, his whip-smart sense of humor—one of the things I most loved was his ability to be present and savor the beautiful moments in his day.

I remember walking with him and his little Scottie dog Mac around the wooded park where we lived.

"Remember to look up to the skies," he would tell my seven-year-old, busy little self. "Remember to stop and look up at the clouds and the stars."

On those walks, he would point out blue jays, cardinals, and squirrels, the pattern that the shadows from the tree branches above made on the path in front of us. Simple things that I ran past every day, which now, in that moment when he pointed them out, felt magical and enchanting.

Use all of your senses to bask in the details

What if, the next time you are gifted with a wonderful memory, instead of pushing it aside for other thoughts, you paused for a moment and ***basked*** *in it? Use all of your senses to notice or remember the details.*

The other day my grandfather popped up on Erised. He was sitting on the porch swing of that beloved old cottage, his face lit up with that warm, welcoming Grandpa smile. I stopped for a moment and closed my eyes, allowing myself to remember the warmth of that summer breeze on my young skin, the painterly light of the sun dappling through the green of one hundred-year-old oak and sycamore trees, the sounds of his laugh and the chattering of woodland birds in the background, the bang of the screen door slamming shut on its hinges behind me, the heft of the porch's painted wooden planks under my bare feet, the clean smell of mountain air, and evergreens, and tiger lilies.

What are the daily rituals that you savor? Or could savor, if you only paused a moment or two longer?

* My cousin loves her English Breakfast tea in the morning. She makes a morning ritual of steeping the tea leaves and savoring it from a beautiful china teacup that belonged to her grandmother.

* My friend Rhonda loves to watch the sunrise over the ridge from her front porch or bedroom window. There are times in the summer when you'll find her enjoying the view from her vegetable garden, often while she's still in her PJs.

* My neighbor loves the nighttime ritual of giving her three-year-old daughter a bath. "My favorite part," she shares, "is when I wrap her in a big, fluffy towel and sit her on my lap, and we sing this little sleepy-time song together. I look forward to that every evening."

* My husband loves the sound of mourning doves. They remind him of a wonderful vacation we took when we'd hear them as we took our morning walk every day. When we hear them now, wherever we are, he will stop and say, "Listen." And we do.

* Another friend's ninety-eight-year-old mother has always loved to paint. Since the onset of Alzheimer's, she no longer can. So now, she colors. He buys her coloring books and crayons in bulk, and they sit down after dinner and savor the time they spend coloring together. Occasionally they even try to stay within the lines.

"A paradox:
The things you don't need to live—books, art, cinema, wine, and so on—are the things you need to live."
—Matt Haig, *The Humans*

The pandemic forced us to shake up our routines and become creative about doing the things that we love. For many of us, time slowed down, giving us a chance to savor and appreciate the small moments as perhaps we haven't in a while. We found new ways to savor the things that are important to us. We took virtual guitar lessons and painting classes, we attended virtual concerts and magic shows. We sat in lawn chairs with the neighbors in the front yard, yelled out our congratulations to the graduate in drive-by celebrations, and wore party hats on-screen to virtually celebrate birthdays and anniversaries. I hope that, now that we've returned to the normal breakneck pace most of us live by, we will remember and savor these small, meaningful moments, and seek them out.

Do you remember a moment that you wished would never end? A moment you wanted to bottle and save, so you could take it out whenever you wanted to and savor it all over again? These moments are the magic that makes our lives rich.

So why not slow down and savor them now?

When I look at those photos on our frame, of the ones that made the cut, there is a theme. In every one of these photographs, we were taking a moment to *savor* life, with all of its many small, rich, and joyful moments.

Remember to stop and look up at the stars.

The Garden

Tonight we are in the garden.
We'll pour a glass of wine.
The soft night air will kiss our cheek, and life will seem so fine.

The lights are twinkling like the stars. They're not as bright but not as far.
Our souls are quieted like our schemes. All gives way to pleasant dreams.

Moments like this don't come often.
They take life's rough edges and simply soften.

Let's just allow the same night air, to soothe away the daily care.
We'll share some time with loving friends, and wish the night would never end.

"Whimsy," by Marian Denny

Happiness Practice

1. What are the things that bring you joy? Not just the Big Things, but the small things?

2. What are the daily rituals that you savor? Or could savor if you only paused a moment or two longer?

3. What is one beloved memory that you treasure? Savor it with all of your senses:

   * *How did you feel?*
     -
     -
   * *How did it smell?*
     -
     -
   * *How did it taste?*
     -
     -

✷ *What did you hear?*

-
-

✷ *What did you see?*

-
-

✷ *How do you feel now?*

-
-

21. Stand Up Straight

"The mind shapes the body. And the body shapes the mind."
—Dr. Amy Cuddy, PhD

The other day, Tim walked into my office and stopped cold. "Let me guess," he said. You're having a tough day."

"Is it that obvious?" I asked.

"Uh, yeah. Look at how you're sitting."

I was slouched over my computer, both elbows on my desk, head down, forehead resting in my hands. I sat up, straightened my shoulders, and rolled my eyes, a little irked. Mostly because I knew he was right. And, sure enough, I immediately felt a little more energized, a smidge more focused, like I might even be able to start chipping away at the pile of work stacked in front of me.

Studies have shown that posture and body language affect performance. According to the NIH, our *"emotion systems prepare us to meet challenges encountered in the environment by adjusting the activation of the cardiovascular, skeletomuscular, neuroendocrine, and autonomic nervous system."*

But you don't need a research report to know this. Have you ever felt your heart pounding with excitement, anticipating a meeting with a new love interest? Have you ever felt your hands sweat or tremble before an important interview?

We allow our *emotions* to change our *physiology*—our body posture, expressions, and breathing.

* We feel sad or down, and guess what? Our shoulders, chest, head, eyes—all down.
* We feel certain and confident and, yep—shoulders up, held head high, breathing steady, and gaze direct.

Do you know what the really cool thing is?

We can also allow our *physiology* to change our *emotions.*

This emotion-body connection works in the reverse order as well. How we use our bodies, breathing, and facial expressions can change our emotions—including our levels of confidence, well-being, and yes, happiness.

What's the body language of a confident, happy person?

Watch any athlete, and you can visibly observe them putting their game face on. Even with an untrained eye, you can see the transformation the instant it happens, can't you?

* A gymnast squares her shoulders, focuses her gaze, and takes a deep breath before launching into the air.
* A swimmer pauses, sets his mouth firmly, and gives a gritty stare at the exact spot where he will dive into the pool.

We can also see the lack of confidence. We see the physical hesitation, pursing of the lips, the questioning eyebrows, the tight facial expressions. Observe enough of these signs, and you can put money on what the outcome will be.

To be happy, act happy

Sometimes we just have to "fake it 'til we make it." Confronted with a big challenge, our brains can put the brakes on: "*Nope. That looks really painful. Not gonna do it.*"

When that happens, we can use our body to *lead* our brain by sending it physical happiness and confidence cues: a deep breath here, a straighter posture there, direct eye contact, a smile.

Speaking of smiling, the journal *Psychological Bulletin* published the results of a study of 11,000 people worldwide on the impact of smiling on our mood. They found that "*smiling makes us feel happier, scowling makes us feel angrier, and frowning makes us feel sadder.*"

Surprised? Didn't think so.

I love watching resilient people decide to lean in. Just like watching an athlete, you can see the moment they put their game face on.

As a performer, Tim has had to train himself to be good at this. The day his mother died, he was scheduled to do a magic performance for 250 people who had flown in from all over the country for a conference. Now, like all of us in any situation, he had choices. In this case, he could:

1. **Cancel**—an understandable option, but one that left an agent, a client, and 250 travel-weary guests in the lurch

2. **Go through the motions**—just get through the show, and let his justifiably mournful emotional state carry over into a lackluster performance

3. **Decide, stand up straight, and lean in**—put his sorrow aside for an hour and channel his emotional best to give his audience an entertaining and magical experience

He chose Door #3.

"How did you ever get through it?" I asked, greeting him with a heartfelt hug that evening.

"It wasn't as hard as I thought it would be," he said as he hugged me back. "I took a really deep breath and stood tall and proud like my mom would have wanted. I thought about all the times she drove me all over town to magic lectures when I was a kid. She took me to my very first gig, when I was 12 years old."

"What was that?" I asked.

"It was at a KOA campground," he smiled thoughtfully, savoring the memory. "They paid me $25 and told me to expect 20 people. But it was a Saturday night, 4th of July weekend, and I was the only game in town."

"Wow!"

"Yeah, there must have been 900 people there. I had to stand on a ping-pong table with my head in the rafters just so they could see me. My dad was so nervous he almost threw up.

But mom hooted and applauded like I was David Copperfield. She was my biggest fan. Until you."

I hugged him harder.

"I felt her in the audience today, cheering me on. This one was for her."

Now, if you break it down, there was an actual process that Tim went through to tap into his best on a difficult day. In fact, we all use this same process, consciously or not, for channeling our Inner Rock Star.

It's got a catchy name and everything:

The Process for Channeling Your Inner Rock Star

1. **Decide**

2. **Change Your Body:** Stand up straight, chest up, strike your rock-star or your super-hero pose, set your face, breathe deep. Let this little jolt of energy from shifting your body help you to:

3. **Change Your Thoughts:** Focus that voice in your head. What's it saying?

   "I can't do this."
   "This is impossible."

   Change the message to a better one:
   "Once I get started, it always goes well."
   "I've GOT this."
   "It's not about me. It's about them."

You know how to do this. You've done this before.

Maybe you've had to square your shoulders before stepping on stage for a presentation or walk into an office for an important meeting or interview. Maybe you've had to straighten your spine and stand a little taller to have a tough conversation with your partner or parent or child or boss. The trick is to be more *intentional* about practicing this happiness skill so that you build that muscle memory.

Let me share a tip that has often helped me stand up straight and step up to a challenge.

First, did you know that, according to a Gallup poll, 40% of Americans are afraid of speaking in public? It's #2 on the list of Things People are Afraid of, right after fear of snakes. When I coach professionals on their public-speaking skills, I share this advice that my sophomore professor of Speech Communications gave to me:

"That rush you feel when you're about to walk on stage? The pounding heart, butterflies in your stomach, dry mouth . . . ? That's adrenalin that you're feeling, your body's Fight or Flight response. So, you have a choice:

1. You can feel that energy and think, 'Oh, no! This is anxiety!' and let that feeling feed your anxiety.

2. Or you can appreciate the fact that your body is gifting you with an extra bonus shot of energy to help you in that moment. And you can channel that energy and use it for an even more engaging, powerful outcome."

In other words: *Welcome the Butterflies.*

That little nugget is *gold*, and it has helped me immeasurably in my career and in life, whether I'm confronted with a big presentation or an MTST *(Most Terrible and Stressful Thing.)*

Try this:

The next time you're feeling frustrated, or a little down, or angry—check your body and your posture. What's it doing?

- Are your facial muscles tense or relaxed?
- Are you breathing fast and shallow, or steady and deep?
- Are your shoulders and chest slumped and down, or held high and back?

If you notice your body slumped and down—bring it back up! A little trick I learned from yoga is to imagine a string connected to your chest, pulling you up. That motion alone will automatically put you in a more positive physiological state. It's pretty magical how changing your posture, breathing, and stance can quickly help you shift your mindset.

And while you're at it, MOVE.

It's been said that sitting is the new smoking. We *know* we need to move our bodies for physical and mental health. Yet, we get so caught up in our work, much of it virtual these days, that we need alarms and gadgets to remind ourselves to stand up and move.

Whether you take a short, brisk walk outside or hit the gym for a good sweat, do you ever regret it? Seriously, do you ever wish you could have that time back? Do you ever think, *"Geez, that was 60 minutes lost. Shoulda spent it on the couch."*

Of course not. Not EVER.

Moving lifts our mood. When possible, there's nothing like taking a quick break to walk outside to allow the movement of your body to change your mood. (*See? Yet another reason to have a dog!)* The combination of the change of scenery, fresh air, and physical movement does wonders to clear the head. It's a Three-fer. And if you look for them, there are always those moments of grace to ***savor*** when we are out and about. When I take the time to do this, I always come back to the moment or task at hand with a fresh perspective and renewed energy. How about you?

Okay, you got this. Whatever your thing is—walking, working out, playing sports, digging dirt and planting things—find something you love to do that clears your head, lifts up your mood, and energizes you.

And stand up straight.

Happiness Practice

The next time you're feeling frustrated, or a little down, or angry—check yourself:

1. What is the voice in your head saying?
   -
   -
   -

2. How is your posture, breathing, facial expression?

   ✷ Are your facial muscles tense or relaxed?
   -
   -
   -

   ✷ Are you breathing fast and shallow, or steady and deep?
   -
   -
   -

   ✷ Are your shoulders and back slumped and down, or held up and back?
   -
   -
   -

3. Change your body:

    * Try straightening your shoulders. Stand tall. Feel that string pulling you up from the chest, higher and lighter.

    * Take a deep breath. Take another.

    * Smile.

    * Okay, now smile even bigger. This time, with your mouth *and* your eyes. You may feel totally dorky (because you kind of are), but that will just make you smile harder. It might even make you laugh!

"Quit slouching and stand up straight!"

—Mom

22. The Habit of Happiness

"No matter what your past has been, you have a spotless future."

—Tony Hsieh

I stopped into a convenience store one morning and stood in line to buy my coffee. The employee behind the cash register greeted her regulars with a smile. Her name tag read "Ann."

"Good Morning, Ralph," Ann said to the man standing in front of her. "How are you today?"

"Better than dead," Ralph grunted. *How does one even respond to that?*

"Well," Ann replied, showing me how it was done, "that is definitely the better option!"

Ralph grumbled off, and the woman behind him stepped up to the register.

"Good Morning. How's it going?" Ann asked.

"This complete *idiot* cut me off and almost broadsided me! What a jerk! I can already tell it's going to be one of those days."

Ann gave her an empathetic look as an elderly man, bent over a cane but dressed impeccably in a pressed shirt and khakis, stepped up to the register.

"Hi, Lou. How are you today?"

"Faaan-tastic!" Lou grinned, "But don't worry, it's early. I'm getting even better!" He said this with a sparkle in his eye and a smile so genuine and infectious that Ann and I both found ourselves smiling back.

"Wow," I said when I took my place in front of Ann at the register, "Lou certainly has a great attitude."

"You have no idea," Ann shook her head. "He lost his wife of 60 years a few months ago, just as he was recovering from a heart attack. He said sometimes he doesn't want to get out of bed in the morning, but he's here every morning at 6:30 for coffee. Somehow, he always seems to find a reason to smile. He told me he and his wife worked hard to be happy in life and that he's not about to give up now."

I left that convenience store with a smile and extended it to the busy-looking woman rushing in the door as I exited. She hesitated a second; then her face warmed, and she smiled back.

The experience made me think. *What is it about people like Lou, who stay upbeat and resilient, despite great emotional and physical pain?*

How we live our days is how we live our lives.

It all comes back to making a very conscious decision to be happy and taking specific actions to support that decision. Lou had built up some pretty strong happiness-muscle memory. It gave him the strength he needed to do the heavy lifting when life got tough and maybe, just maybe, shine a little light on those around him.

He wasn't pushing down or repressing his feelings.
He wasn't being naive or cavalier or blindly optimistic.
"He worked hard to be happy in his life, and he's not about to give up now."

It's the actions we take every day that lead us down our path in life. Often, by making even one small change over time, we can gain powerful positive momentum to propel us forward, toward our desired outcome.

There's a Magic Formula for creating positive momentum that's based on my observations of what happier, more successful people do.

Ready for it?

Creating momentum requires consistently doing *more* of the things that move us forward, toward our goals, and *fewer* of the things that hold us back.

That's it. Creating momentum in our lives is actually pretty simple.

- Do we focus on the traffic and the crappy weather on our commute?

- Or do we listen to our favorite music or podcast, and savor the warmth of our morning coffee?

At any moment, we can decide and take small actions to shift momentum to support the life we want. The key is *consistency*. We talked earlier about how happiness is like a muscle. The more you consciously decide to use it, the stronger your happiness-muscle memory becomes, and the more resilient you will be when those storm clouds roll in.

When was a time in your life when you had positive momentum?

- ✷ Maybe you were training for a marathon or nailing it at tennis or golf.
- ✷ Maybe your garden flourished with all the attention you gave it that year.
- ✷ Maybe you were eating healthy foods, working out, and strengthening your body.

Can you think of a time? *So, how did you do it?* Remember the Power Momentum Process we talked about in **Progress**? There's a three-step process we all use for gaining momentum, consciously or unconsciously:

Step 1: Decide—Resolve to think and do something (even one, small thing) a little differently

Step 2: Act—Take frequent, small, consistent actions every day until you make progress toward your goal (aka develop a habit)

Step 3: Forgive yourself—When you fall off the wagon, get right back on track, even more resolved this time

Developing the Habit of Happiness is no different.

What if you decided on just *one small shift* to tap into more joy in your life? Remember, the definition of "happiness" for *Decide Happy* is to gain a greater sense of:

Love and connection—in your relationships with people, animals, nature, yourself, and the world around you

Peacefulness and calm—an inner strength, state of presence, and well-being; that sense of gratitude and "I've got this," no matter what life throws at you

Contribution and making a difference—leaving the day and your corner of the world a little bit better than how you found it

Moving forward—the feeling of making progress emotionally and physically, moving on purpose toward your goals

So, where do you want to begin?

Each chapter in this book gives you a place to start. Choose one that works for you.

* What if you responded with more energy and joy when someone asks, "How are you doing?"

* What would your day be like if you started it with a calm mind and grateful heart by **clearing the clutter** with your Daily Ten?

* What if you noticed the small things that make you smile and resolved to take a moment to **savor** and celebrate them?

* How good would it feel to take some specific action, large or small, to make **progress** toward a goal or dream you've been nurturing?

* What might the impact be if you took a moment to show a **kindness** to a neighbor or friend or stranger?

* What if, instead of beating yourself up so much, you were **gentle with yourself** and treated yourself like you were your own, dearest, very best friend throughout your life?

* Can you imagine what life would feel like if you trained yourself to default to a more positive **meaning?** And assumed positive intent from another? Could there be a silver lining, an unexpected gift in your MTST (*Most Terrible and Stressful Thing*)?

* What if you challenged an old version of your **identity** that no longer served you? And adopted a braver, happier one instead?

* What would it mean if you resolved to use more empowering **words**—both with others and in your own head?

* What if you decided that, for today, or maybe this week, you will **focus** on the beauty of another person or the world around you, instead of the fault?

* How powerful would it feel for you to focus on what you *can* **control**, instead of on all the things you can't?

* What would it mean to you and your loved ones if you decided to **be there when you're there** with them in the moment and not distracted by something else?

* Or you surrounded yourself with **Your People** who lift you up, and distanced yourself from those who consistently bring you down?

* What impact would it have to chip away at a heavy stack of negatives by **stacking up** the positives in your day?

* How amazing would it feel to **clean up a mess** and repair a relationship? What would it mean to have that person more present in your life?

- ✷ How rich could life be if you allowed yourself to fully **feel it all?**

- ✷ What would the impact be on your future if you decided to **let go** of the pain you've let drag you down for years?

- ✷ What if you decided to **stand up straight** and meet challenge or adversity eye to eye, knowing that you already have all of the strength, wisdom, and resourcefulness to handle it with grace?

- ✷ And how much joy would life hold for you if you began or ended each day with acknowledging three things, big or small, that you are truly **grateful** for?

- ✷ And what do you think could happen in your life if you stacked a few of these skills and practices for more focus, more momentum, more joy?

Who could you become?

This book began with a story.

That morning on the front porch with my mom, when I promised her I was going to "Be Fine," she couldn't know the outcome of the diagnosis any more than I did. And she certainly wasn't asking me to put on a brave face and blindly swear I was going to be okay, as if saying the words would magically make those rampant cells stop dividing.

But she *was* asking me to make a decision.

She was challenging me to step up and believe that, even though I had no control over that diagnosis, I had a choice about my response to it. If I didn't begin this difficult journey believing that I had this choice, then it was already over. If I had let fear take control, the experience would have been infinitely more painful for me and my loved ones, regardless of the physical outcome.

None of us has a crystal ball. There's no way to know what the future will be. As far as any of us knows, we get one life.

Life is finite.

Age is a *privilege*.

But until we take that last breath, we are *alive*.

We make choices every day, all day long. How will you choose to live your days? By giving up? Or by stepping up? By letting the events of life toss you around, unmoored or angry or afraid? Or by taking control of that fantastic miracle of a brain you have and deciding that *you* are the leader of your life? *You* control the soundtrack that plays in your head and the actions you take that impact your life and everyone around you.

The common denominator in every experience you will ever have in your entire life is YOU.

Dear friend, you are a worthy human being, who has every right to be here, as much as the sky and the sun and the clouds and the trees and the stars. You deserve the peace of mind that comes from adopting a happiness mindset. You have a right and an obligation to the world to be your *most loving, calm, contributing, moving-forward* best.

I hope you find these skills a gentle reminder from a friend on her own journey to **Do** what you **Know.** My deepest wish for you is that you take the time to stop and reflect on these practices to remember why you are here, what's most important to you, and that you always have choices.

Our emotions, like our character, are not fixed. Every day is a fresh start. Every day brings 24 shiny, new hours to live. You already have the power. You have the strength. You have the resourcefulness. You have everything you need. Right here. Right now.

On any day, at any moment, you can *Decide.*

Happiness Practice

If you don't like where you are emotionally in life, then move. You are not a tree.

Here is a powerful little "stealth" exercise to build momentum called **"Start. Stop. Continue."**

It's "stealth" because it's super simple. And, when you actually DO it, it's crazy effective. It helps to be specific. Don't just write, "I'm going to look at the positive side of things." *What are you specifically going to do?*

Here's how it works:

1. What's one thing that you're going to **Start** doing as a result of reading this book?
   -
   -

- ✷ If you like, refer to the summary questions in this chapter.
- ✷ Or, check out the Decide Happy Quick reference guide to dust off your memory.
- ✷ Take your time with this. Okay, got it? Now write it down. Here's the perfect spot:

2. What's one thing you're going to **Stop** doing? Write it down.
   -
   -

3. What's one thing you're doing now that is working that you are going to **Continue**? Write it down.
   -
   -

   ✷ Why is this important to you?
   -
   -
   -
   -
   -

   ✷ What do you stand to gain when you start, stop, or continue doing these things?
   -
   -
   -
   -

- What do you lose if you don't?
  -
  -
  -
  -

- How will this decision—and the actions you subsequently take—impact the ones you love?
  -
  -
  -
  -

- What ripple effect might that have? On your family, your circle, your community?
  -
  -
  -
  -

You can find me at DecideHappy.com and also subscribe to *A Little Bit of Happy in Your Inbox* once or twice a month.

I'm so excited for you and this next chapter in your journey. I would love to hear from you!

"Most folks are about as happy as they make up their minds to be."

—Abraham Lincoln

Sometimes miracles are just good people with kind hearts

I've always found the happiest people to be the most generous—with their knowledge, talents, and time, as well as their finances.

Giving makes us happy.

A generous portion of proceeds from *Decide Happy* benefits awesome causes like:

* Mental Health and Wellness—in our magnificent, tumultuous, ever-changing world, we all need to work a little more intentionally to keep our thoughts calm, positive, and strong
* The Chordoma Foundation - a mighty little foundation making a huge contribution to the world to find a cure for rare cancers, save lives (including mine), and support quality of life for survivor-thrivers
* Animal Rescue—because animals just make us happy

I'm always interested in supporting great causes. Please contact me at DecideHappy.com to learn more about speaking, workshops, and fundraising engagements to help your awesome mission.

Happiness is a constant decision.
And at any moment, you can decide.

Susan

Acknowledgments

For My People

To Tim, for being my #1 fan, cheering me on from the front row, and for loving every evolution of me. And for your unwavering conviction that, even on my Most Terrible of Days, I am still a "solar flare."

To my beloved Unicorns—Charmaine, Linda, CJ and my Smith cousins—Sandy, Kit and Dianne, who offered constant and never-ending encouragement, no matter how many times you read that questionable paragraph or obsessed with me over fonts and cover art.

And to Dale, Janis, Kristin, and Corey—for courageously sharing your critical and/or aesthetic eye to help me make *Decide Happy* even better.

A heartfelt thank you to Susie Rinehart, who helped me strengthen my voice, and challenges me to err on the side of brave over perfect every day.

To my fellow authors, Brian Bartes, David McNally, Chris Malone—who shared your book-writing journeys so graciously and generously, and let me stand on your ample shoulders to see the lay of the land ahead.

To Bob and Holly Parks and Andrea McOwen, for championing me, my mission, and making it possible to bring my whole person to my work and do what I love every day.

To my Home Team, my family, for so much fun. And for letting me use your hilarious stories, even when they involved the occasional misdemeanor. And to Mom and Dad, who gave me wings and never once doubted that I would fly.

To Michele, Ronda, and the creative team at 1106 Design, who immediately saw my vision and encouraged me to run fast and far with it.

To the Universe, for preparing me for this. And for inspiring me to channel the best and the worst of my story, with the hope of making life's journey a little more joyful for someone else.

And to all of you reading this, including My People whom I have not yet met. Because of you I feel an even greater responsibility to be my most *loving, calm, contributing, moving-forward* best in the world.

For that and for all of you, I am supremely grateful.

About the Author

Susan Hall is an author, speaker, and professional performance coach. For twenty-five years, she has helped Fortune 500 companies and thousands of people learn the mindset and skills needed for better results—in business and in life.

Susan is also a slightly obsessed animal lover, globe-trotter, artist, and fitness enthusiast, and still has an avid crush on Tim, her husband of 30 years. She lives in Baltimore, MD and Delray Beach, FL with Tim and their two (sometimes three) rescue dogs.

Decide Happy's mission is to help people be their *most loving, calm, contributing, moving-forward best.* Susan takes this mission far more seriously than she takes herself.

Find out more and sign up to receive *A Little Bit of Happy* in your inbox once or twice a month at

DecideHappy.com